TODAY'S ANNUITY PRODUCTS -
A TOOL TO CREATE PROTECTED LIFETIME INCOME

THE
FINANCIAL
VERSE

HARRY N. STOUT

TABLE OF CONTENTS

PLEASE READ BEFORE YOU PROCEED

The FinancialVerse book series has been written to present financial concepts, insurance, tax, and basic financial information and ideas in a condensed, simple-to-understand manner. This was done to educate the reader and allow the reader to obtain a general understanding of the key financial challenges and decisions they will face in their life's journey.

The *FinancialVerse*, its author, and affiliated companies have not received any sponsorship or compensation from any of the organizations referenced in this book.

References to specific tax regulations, dollar limits, or regulatory restrictions were current as of the time of publication. As is the case in our fast-moving world, things change. The reader should make sure they have the most current information before they chose to take action on a particular idea presented in this book.

Before making any major financial decision or taking related financial actions, it is suggested that the reader consult a qualified financial professional who has been licensed to provide this information, needed service, or sell the requested financial products.

This informational publication is designed to provide general information on the subjects covered. Pursuant to Internal Revenue Circular 230, it is not, however, intended to provide specific legal or tax advice and cannot be used to avoid tax penalties or to promote, market, or recommend any tax plan or arrangement. Please note that the FinancialVerse, its affiliated companies, and their representatives and employees do not give financial planning, legal or tax advice. As written in this book, the reader is encouraged to consult a licensed financial professional, tax advisor or attorney on these matters.

Thank you for purchasing this FinancialVerse book and investing in your financial literacy.

FOREWORD

The financial universe—or the **FinancialVerse** as I call it—is made up of the knowledge, decisions, resources, risks, and tools that an individual encounters in their life's financial journey. I believe most people, regardless of background and level of education, do not fundamentally understand the financial universe such that they can successfully navigate the key financial decisions and risks they will face in life. Arming themselves with at least a basic knowledge of what they will encounter and how to go about making informed decisions will enable the traveler to reach a level of success well beyond what they thought possible.

The Value of This Book

I have spent 20 years of my career in the annuity business in the United States, and around the globe. I have served several large annuity businesses in various roles like product developer, chief marketing officer, and chief executive officer. In the spirit of full disclosure, I own several of these products. That is, I eat my own cooking.

What I have realized in the course of my career, is that once consumers understand the protections and tax advantages of annuity products and carefully look at the financial risks they face in aging, including outliving their savings, they come to realize that annuity products are a great tool in providing solutions to address these challenges. I wanted to write a book to clearly present the key aspects of these products, how they work, along with a full rundown of their positives and negatives. I wanted the book to be focused and easy to read. I wanted to present the major points of knowledge such that the reader, once they read the book, would feel comfortable meeting with a financial professional to determine if the product was a tool they should use in their overall financial plan.

As you read and listen to the mainstream financial media, there is no investment or insurance strategy that draws more conflicting opinions from financial professionals than the purchase and use of annuity products. You will hear and read that some people hate all types of annuities, others only hate certain types, while other financial professionals love them as do their clients. I wanted to write a book that objectively presents the facts about this misunderstood product and that after reading its content, you, the consumer, could decide if the product is a tool that fits into your life in the FinancialVerse.

My belief is that annuities are a fundamental tool that can be used to minimize certain financial risks. Like any tool, they should only be used when appropriate. They are not for everyone nor do they solve all financial problems.

This book, third in the FinancialVerse Series (www.financialverse.com), presents that knowledge and a framework to help the reader understand this often overlooked and underused income-creation tool. We will look at how to use today's annuity products in protecting against important financial risks. I will be your financial Sherpa as you travel through the world of annuities. My ideas are based on my experience and take into account today's longer lifespans, economic trends, and how we manage our lives as we age.

To begin with, how would you answer the following:

- ➤ Do you understand how annuities work?

- ➤ Do you know the major reasons why annuities are purchased?

➤ Did you know that, as of year-end 2017, over 199 million Americans already own an annuity and may not realize they do?

➤ Did you know that in recent years there have been significant innovations to improve the consumer benefits of these products?

➤ Did you know there is no limit to the number of annuities you can own that are purchased with after-tax dollars?

➤ Did you know annuities provide tax-advantaged benefits?

➤ Did you know annuities can provide cash to help pay for the costs of a terminal illness or nursing home care?

➤ Did you know there are very few consumer complaints about annuity products?

➤ Did you know there are special annuities that can be structured to provide supplemental income after age 85?

➤ Did you know annuities can be a source of emergency cash throughout your life?

If your answers to most of these questions is no, you are not unlike the majority of Americans when it comes to understanding how to use today's annuity products for protection against financial risks and how to make use of their inherent tax advantages. Overall, consumers don't understand the value of the products and the protections they provide against a number of common financial risks.

It is now time to become better aware of these products and how they can play an important role in managing the key financial risks you face. You should not be fearful of trying to understand this product. It is all about common sense. This book will help you understand the basic products, costs, benefits, and limitations of annuities, and I will try to make the subject as easy to understand as possible. After you are done reading this book, you should have a basic understanding of annuities and how to use them in your life. You can then take the necessary steps to purchase the product that best meets your needs and buying preference.

I am here to help you by providing practical thoughts and ideas on how to understand and use this financial tool. The objective of the FinancialVerse book series, is to help you live an anxiety-free financial life. I will offer you simple, proven ideas, and practical insights based on my 20+ years of experience in the annuity business.

CHAPTER 1

WHAT ARE ANNUITIES AND HOW DO THEY WORK?

WHAT ARE ANNUITIES?

Annuities are legal contracts between a state-regulated life insurance company and the purchaser, who is referred to as the contract's owner. The annuity contract consists of a core contract, and add-ons called riders that make up the entire agreement. In their most basic form, in exchange for a cash amount, called a premium, annuities guarantee that payments will be made over a time period and at a frequency (i.e., monthly, quarterly or annually) that the contract owner elects. The annuity contract spells out all guaranteed payments and benefits to be provided, and what conditions and related costs must exist for the payments and benefits to be made. The primary purpose of annuities is to provide supplemental, guaranteed or protected income for the latter years of life.

There are normally four parties to the annuity contract:

1. *The Life Insurance Company* – This is the company that issues the policy and is contractually required to keep all the promises made in the contract.

2. *The Annuitant* – This is the individual (it must be an individual) whose life is used to calculate the annuity payments to be made.

3. *The Beneficiary* – This is the party who will receive any death or other benefits payable under the annuity.

4. *The Owner* – This is the individual or entity (the owner does not need to be a natural person) that has all of the ownership rights (i.e., cash withdrawal or surrender rights) under the contract.

KEY CHARACTERISTICS

The major characteristics of annuity products are:

➤ They are legal contracts sold by state-domiciled and regulated life insurance companies.

➤ The products possess certain tax advantages including tax deferral from current taxation on income, earned by the contract.

➤ Congress and the Internal Revenue Service understand that annuities are products used primarily to produce supplemental income later in life and have given annuity products certain tax advantages. They did so to create incentives to save for this objective and have placed certain restrictions on annuity contracts because of their tax-advantaged status. These restrictions relate to the taxation of withdrawals, contract gains, death benefits, and living benefits. A specific example is the tax penalty normally levied if the earnings from the annuity contract are withdrawn before the annuitant reaches age 59 and a half. Such early withdrawals are subject to regular income tax on the earnings plus a 10% tax penalty. There are certain limited exceptions for avoiding this penalty, but I will not go into them at this time.

➤ You can buy two types of annuities: immediate (begin payments right away, e.g., $500 per month within 30 days of purchase), or deferred (payments begin later).

➤ Most of the annuities have no upfront sales charges. The full deposit to an annuity goes to work, earning money right away. Annuities do have surrender or withdrawal fees that the insurance company will keep if money is withdrawn within a certain period, usually 5 to 7 years, after the annuity is purchased. These fees are in addition to any taxes, or tax penalties, that may be due when money is taken out of an annuity prematurely.

➤ A unique feature of annuities is the different income options available. An immediate income annuity pays a regular income, usually monthly, to the annuitant. A deferred annuity can be converted to an immediate income annuity, or a lump sum of money from another source can be used to purchase an immediate income annuity. Income options include a protected income stream that will last as long as the annuitant is alive (i.e., lifetime income). Other income options combine lifetime income with survivor income for a spouse or a guarantee of income for a certain number of years if the annuitant does not live that long. Immediate income annuities can also be set up to pay an income for a set period of time, such as 10 or 20 years.

Once an income is selected, however, it cannot be changed. An annuity owner also has the option to withdraw the money as a lump sum from a deferred annuity rather than selecting an immediate income annuity payout option.

➤ Annuity contracts can be purchased with after-tax dollars (a non-qualified annuity) or with pre-tax dollars (a qualified annuity). In Chapter 3 we will discuss the taxation of annuity products. There is **no limit** on the amount of annuity products that can be purchased with after-tax dollars. **There are certain special rules or restrictions on the amount of annuity products that can be purchased in one year from one insurance carrier that require that these annuity purchases be aggregated for taxation purposes.** This is referred to in the industry as the serial annuity rule.

➤ You can purchase an annuity by making a single premium payment (e.g., $25,000) or by making a number of payments on a periodic basis such as monthly (e.g., $200 per month). The latter type is called a flexible premium annuity.

➤ Annuities earn interest in three major ways: 1) through a fixed return provided by the insurance carrier (e.g., 2% per year), 2) through a fixed return tied to an external index (fixed indexed annuity), or 3) a variable return (a variable return is generated by investing in designated stock and bond funds). Some annuity contracts allow for the amount in the contract to be invested in different options: fixed or variable.

➤ Gains on annuity contracts are taxed as ordinary income and not as capital gain. This treatment is tied to the fact that

Congress has given the tax-deferral advantage to these products.

➤ There are six major annuity product types: fixed, variable, fixed indexed, buffered or structured, immediate income annuities, and deferred income annuities. We will discuss these major product types as well as the number of different products available as part of each category in Chapter 4.

The above are the key characteristics of annuity products, and we will explain many of these in more detail later in this book.

BRIEF HISTORY OF ANNUITIES

The origin of today's annuity products dates back to Roman times. In this section, I will give you a brief ride through annuity history and highlight for you key events and developments. You will see that these products have existed in some form for hundreds of years.

In the financial history books, the first annuities can be found referenced in the time before Christ and played a role in the Roman Empire. The word annuity has a Latin basis and stems from the word, "annua," meaning for payments made yearly or recurring annually. Roman soldiers received payment in the form of annuities for their military service.

Annuities are also mentioned in the Middle Ages and were used by feudal lords to help cover the cost of warfare. They were funded by individuals who were offered large amounts of cash that went to the surviving investor in the form of tontines. Tontines were named for their creator, a Neapolitan financier, named Lorenzo Tonti. Tontine arrangements were eventually outlawed because they encouraged the death of investors so that their interests would be redistributed among the remaining investors.

Annuities made their initial appearance in the American colonies in the late 1700s as a means for religious groups to provide a secure retirement for ministers and their families. They were set up such that the sponsoring church promised to pay a lifetime income in return for contributions made by the ministers. At the time of the War of 1812, annuities, finally, became available to the public as a private financial instrument when a Pennsylvania insurance company began to issue individual annuities.

The financial turmoil and uncertainty of the Great Depression of the 1930s helped annuities gain popularity. The uncertain economic environment triggered a huge demand for annuities by individuals and families that were concerned that their bank would become insolvent. To many investors it became apparent that life insurance companies offered more financial security and stability than their banking institutions. These people wanted their future incomes to be as secure as possible.

At the same time, the U.S. government wanted the public to become more financially aware in an effort to manage during this uncertain time. The government's goal was to incent individuals to save. The concern spawned the creation of corporate-sponsored retirement annuities, or pension plans, that energized the individual annuity industry. As part of this legislation, tax deferral was provided for qualified retirement plans including annuities. The popularity of annuities continued to grow as individuals took advantage of the tax-deferred nature of these products.

Until the 1950s, the only annuity products available were those offering fixed designs. In 1952, variable annuities (those whose return was tied to the performance of the equity markets) were introduced. Instead of a fixed rate of return, variable annuity rates were derived from the returns on separate investment accounts, which were selected by the annuity owner. These products gained significant popularity and have been a leading product sales category ever since.

During the early 1980s, when inflation, interest rates, and tax rates were at their historical highs, annuities gained broad appeal. Fixed annuity interest rates spiked upward into the mid-teens. With tax rates as high as 70%, money began to flow from taxable savings into annuities.

It was the bull market run of the '80s that catapulted variable annuities into the limelight. The opportunity for higher returns, coupled with the tax deferral on earnings, motivated investors to buy these products. The number of variable annuity products exploded, and annuity sales increased dramatically.

As the equity markets grew, more volatile variable annuities began to lose some of their luster. And as interest rates began their two-decade long march to today's historic lows, fixed annuities became less attractive. To combat these declining sales results, life insurance companies introduced fixed index annuities in the late 1990s as a way for investors to participate in some of the upside of the market while limiting their downside risk. This product category has continued to grow in popularity as a way to deal with market volatility and to obtain returns higher than those available from fixed annuities and fixed investments such as certificates of deposit. Today, fixed index annuities are the largest selling fixed annuity product type.

As time progressed and consumer needs relating to aging became more evident, additional consumer benefits were added to the products. These benefits included alternatives to contract annuitization (e.g., lifetime withdrawal benefits), nursing home confinement benefits and new benefits were added to help pay for long-term care events, enhanced death benefits, and emergency cash needs. In recent years, Qualified Lifetime Annuity Contracts (QLACs) or longevity annuity products were introduced in the market. These new products and consumer benefits were announced to help deal with the need to fund the costs of increasing life spans and to minimize related longevity risk.

In the last decade, annuity sales have consistently produced approximately a quarter-of-a-trillion dollars of new sales-per-year based on information provided by the Secure Retirement Institute. The number of annuity products has expanded well into the hundreds, which has resulted in a much greater selection, but it also carries with it a lot of confusion for consumers, trying to find the right product for their needs.

Annuity products, once sold primarily by life insurance agents, are now a product staple of banks, brokerage houses and registered investment advisors. We will discuss where you can buy annuity products in Chapter 9.

Famous Annuity Owners

Famous owners of annuity products, who are referenced as using annuities as part of their financial planning include:

Ben Franklin, one of the founding fathers of our country, left annuities benefiting the cities of Boston and Philadelphia upon his death. For over 200 years, all the way through to the early 1990s, Franklin's annuity to Boston continued paying and only stopped when the city opted to receive the remaining balance in a lump sum distribution.

Babe Ruth, the baseball Hall-of-Famer, is reported to have moved his money into annuities ahead of the Stock Market Crash of 1929 to protect his assets.

The infamous ex-athlete O. J. Simpson was said to have used annuities to protect his income from lawsuits and creditors.

Ben Bernanke, the former head of the Federal Reserve Bank, disclosed in 2006 that two annuity contracts were included amongst his major financial assets.

Annuity products go back hundreds of years in history. They were introduced in the United States in the late 18th century and have grown to be a business that produces more than a quarter-trillion-dollars of new sales each year. Millions of Americans own annuity products as part of their financial assets and income-producing plans.

THE KEY PHASES OF AN ANNUITY

There are two basic phases to an annuity contract: accumulation and payout. Consumers can purchase contracts that have no accumulation period and begin payments immediately–an immediate income annuity–or they can purchase contracts that defer payment for decades–a deferred annuity. Let's look at each phase.

The Accumulation Phase

This phase is the time period when you invest money in the annuity and it accumulates earnings. You can invest in one lump sum (a single premium annuity) or you can invest a series of payments into an annuity (a flexible premium annuity). For flexible premium products, the payments may be of equal size over a number of years (e.g., $300 per month per year for 10 years) or they may consist of a series of variable payments (e.g., $5,000 or $8,000 every other year).

During the accumulation phase, the annuity contract earns interest in a tax-deferred manner. There are three pools of money that earn interest. These are:

1. *The Principal* – The initial and subsequent premium deposits.

2. *The Interest* – Since no current taxes are paid, all interest earned by the contract compounds fully on a pre-tax basis.

3. *The Unpaid Taxes* – Since the contract is tax deferred, the contract-holder earns interest on the taxes that are not paid currently.

Distribution Phase

The second phase of an annuity contract is the distribution phase. This phase is when income is elected to be taken from the contract and disbursed to the contract-holder or annuitant. There are six keyways that cash is distributed from the annuity contract. They include:

1. *Full Surrender of the Contract* – The contract holder can withdraw all of the money in the annuity at any time, subject to the surrender charge provisions of the contract.

2. *Partial Withdrawals* – Partial withdrawals are just that. An amount is withdrawn from the annuity contract that is less than 100% of the contract's value. Most annuity contracts offer the ability to withdraw up to 10% of the annuity's value each year without surrender charges. Amounts withdrawn in excess of the 10% free amount are usually subject to a surrender charge if the annuity is still in the surrender charge period.

3. *Systematic Withdrawals* – This is a method of withdrawing funds from an annuity account by which the annuitant withdraws funds from the account in specified amounts for a specified payment frequency. For example, 7% each year on June 1. If systematic withdrawals are used, they do not guarantee lifelong payments as if the contract holder choses annuitization. With a systematic withdrawal schedule, one chooses instead to withdraw funds from an account until it is emptied, bearing the risk that the funds become depleted before one dies. The advantages of a systematic withdrawal are that the contract holder has flexibility to take payments when desired, stop payments from being made, and control when income taxes are paid on withdrawals. A contract holder choosing this withdrawal

method instead of the annuitization method would not be limited to a small amount of funds every month and could, in fact, remove their funds from the account relatively quickly should they desire to do so. The disadvantages of a systematic withdrawal schedule from an annuity, by not guaranteeing a lifelong income stream for the annuitant, places the risk of a longer-than-expected lifespan on the shoulders of the contract owner instead of on the insurance company offering the annuity.

4. *Annuitization* – Annuitization is the process of converting the accumulated value of a deferred annuity contract into a stream of payments. Once annuitization is elected, the contract stops accumulating as it has been, and a separate payment calculation is made and implemented. There are a number of different payment options that can be selected depending on an individual annuity contract's provisions. These include:

➤ *Lifetime Payments* – The simplest option for annuitization is a lifetime payment. With this option, the insurance company continues to make payments for as long as the annuitant lives–technically until the annuitant dies, which could happen one year after annuitizing or many years later. Generally, this is the better option should the annuitant live a long life. If the annuitant dies shortly after annuitizing, there is no refund of the contract's principal. A lifetime election is just that–for a lifetime and no longer.

➤ *Life with Period Certain* – To guard against the risk of forfeiting all money when the annuitant dies early using a lifetime payment option, you can add a "period certain." With this option, the insurance company will make payments for either the life of the annuitant or the period that is chosen, whichever is longer. For example, you might use a 10-year period certain. In that case, payments will continue for at least 10 years regardless of when the annuitant dies and payments will continue as long as the annuitant is alive, even if that period stretches beyond 10 years. Because you are reducing your risk of an early death, your monthly (or annual) payments will be smaller if you select a life-with-period-certain option as compared to a lifetime payment.

➤ *Joint and Last Survivor* – Some annuity owners want to provide income not just for themselves but also for someone else, such as a spouse. A joint and last survivor payment option will provide income as long as either of the people chosen remains alive. Again, this results in a lower payment than a standard lifetime payment because, with two people, there is a greater likelihood that one of them will live for many years.

➤ Period Certain – You don't necessarily have to use someone's lifetime when you annuitize. If you simply want to get income for a certain number of years (until your Social Security or other income benefits begin, for example), the contract owner can instruct the insurance company to pay the annuitant for a specific number of years. Based on my experience, 20 years is the most popular period consumers select.

➤ *Other Options* – Different insurers offer different options. Talk with your licensed financial professional, or a customer service representative at your life insurance company, to find out about any other options.

For most annuity contracts, annuitizing is an irrevocable decision. Once this option is elected, it is difficult, or even impossible, to go back and rescind the election. This irrevocability is one of the major negatives of electing annuitization. Once elected, the contract holder loses flexibility and control over when payments are received. The reason for this lack of flexibility is that once annuitization is chosen, the insurance company takes steps to manage their risk. They do this by matching investments to the option you have elected by allocating existing assets in its portfolio or purchasing new assets that will fund your election. Once these investments are made, it is difficult, and potentially costly, to unwind them.

5. *Income Riders* – During the past 15 years, the life insurance industry has developed several different types of income riders that can be added to annuity contracts. These riders were developed in order to provide the contract owner with the ability to control the timing and amount of payments without having to annuitize the contract. These riders overcome the major negatives of annuitization. The riders were designed to provide income options for the contract holder that do not require annuitization but provide lifetime income guarantees. The following are the most popular types of income riders:

a) Guaranteed Lifetime Withdrawal Benefit (GLWB)

b) Guaranteed Minimum Income Benefit (GMIB)

a) *Guaranteed Lifetime Withdrawal Benefit (GLWB)*

The most popular supplemental riders sold today are GLWBs. There are separate fees charged for these riders. They are the most simple and straightforward. Simply stated, for various ages, the contract holder is given the option to withdraw a certain percentage of the contract each year for his or her lifetime, regardless of the account running out of cash to pay the withdrawal. For example, if the annuity had a benefit value of $200,000 and the benefit elected at age 70 was 5%, then the annuitant would receive $10,000 per year for the rest of his or her life. If the annuitant lived for 25 years and withdrew $250,000 from the contract, the insurance company would pay the difference of $50,000 out of its own funds. That is the whole idea of having the rider—it is income insurance.

b) *Guaranteed Minimum Income Benefit (GMIB)*

The GMIB rider requires that the investor annuitize before receiving the benefit and may also include time and age limitations. The GMIB provides a set lifetime income upon retirement in exchange for giving up your principal. Investment performance is not a factor. Rather, the payment relies on either the contract value or the investment amount plus an assigned interest rate. The assigned interest rate, which is specified in the annuity contract, is either simple or compounded and is used to provide a basis for calculating the investor's payments.

6. *Living Benefits – Nursing Home or Long-Term Care Protection –* In the event of catastrophic illness or confinement to a care facility, these riders allow contract holders to withdraw funds without penalties, so long as he or she meets certain conditions. The Pension Protection Act of 2006 inspired a series of products combining annuities with long-term care. Since 2010, distributions from annuity contracts to pay for long-term care premiums are tax free, so long as certain criteria are met. Previously, these withdrawals faced a potential 10% penalty if the withdrawals were made prior to age 59-and-a-half and were subject to taxation at ordinary income tax rates.

Living benefit riders offer a way to fortify the fixed income portion of your plan for retirement. They offer a specific defined benefit attached to your annuity, which adds an extra layer of protection. The most important advantage of adding an income rider to an annuity is to allow you to maintain control, and give access to your principal, while being guaranteed a protected lifetime income. As stated above, with the right income rider, you will not have to "annuitize" your principal.

As a reminder, the cost of having an income benefit rider is a deduction from the annuity contract's principal every year in the range of .5% to 1.2%. This charge continues each year until the rider is exercised or dropped from the policy. If you no longer need to have this income option, it is best to notify the insurer of this and request that the deductions be stopped.

UNDERSTANDING THE BASIC BUILDING BLOCKS

There are seven basic building blocks that make up an annuity product that you need to understand as a potential buyer:

1. *Maximum Purchase Amounts* – For annuity contracts purchased with after-tax dollars (i.e., non-qualified annuities) there is no limit to the amount that can be invested. Annuity contracts purchased with pre-tax dollars are subject to the income restrictions and limitations for qualified products such as IRAs and 401(k) plans. These limitations are a major consideration when planning with annuity products.

2. *Interest Earning Strategies* - There are three major ways that interest is earned and credited to annuity contracts. They are:

➤ *Fixed Return* – For fixed return policies, the life insurer pays a fixed return (e.g., 2%) on all cash accumulated in the policy. The life insurer sets the investment strategy for the policy and is responsible for managing all cash accumulated in the policy. The rate of interest earned is usually declared and paid each year and is subject to any contractually declared minimum rates of interest (e.g., 1%) written into the annuity contract. The rate of interest is set by the state approving the product. These policies provide that you will never receive less than the minimum guaranteed rate of interest before any policy charges. Fixed return policies appeal to individuals who want to know what they will earn, and not be subject to any volatile market movements.

➤ *Variable Return* – Variable return policies are considered investment products, which are subject to the securities' laws and regulations. This is because you, the policyholder, are responsible for managing all cash accumulated in the contract by deciding which investments to put the cash into, based on a line-up of options offered by the life insurance company. These investments usually do not guarantee a minimum return to you and, if you chose the wrong investments, you can lose money. You are the investment manager for this product. These products appeal to individuals with a higher risk tolerance, who are willing to be subject to the potential volatility of market movements.

➤ *Indexed Return* – For indexed policies, the cash accumulated in the policy earns a rate of interest based on the results of the performance of an index that the insurance carrier has designated, such as the Standard and Poor's 500 Index of stocks, subject to a minimum annual interest rate guarantee or floor that is usually set at 0% before policy charges and expenses. There are also certain limits on how much of the upside in an index you will get credit for. Also, just how much of the change in the indexed is credited to the policy is subject to the contractual provisions in the policy. These policies are designed to produce returns that are more than a pure fixed return but much less than a full variable return. These products appeal to individuals who have a higher risk tolerance but who do not want to be subject to wild market movements and volatility.

3. *Surrender Charges* – A major component of all deferred annuity contracts is the existence of a surrender charge. A "surrender charge" is a type of sales charge you must pay if you sell or withdraw money from a deferred annuity during the surrender charge period. The surrender charge period is usually defined in the annuity contract, and typically lasts 5 to 7 years after you purchase the annuity. Surrender charges reduce the value of, and the return on, your deposit if you must withdraw cash from the contract. Different annuity products have different surrender charge amounts and periods based on the rate of interest offered to the consumer. Surrender charges are needed by the life insurance company, as they are investing the money supporting the annuity contract primarily into bonds that mature in 7 to 10 years. If you were to withdraw your money from the annuity contract, and interest rates were to have increased, the life insurer would incur a loss of liquidation on the bonds to pay you. Surrender charges are essential to support the interest rate offered by the life insurance company. Some annuity contracts are issued with a return of premium

feature. This feature dictates that no matter when the contract owner requests a full surrender of the annuity contract, they will receive at least the initial deposit they made at the time of the contract. Although, not explicitly stated, there is a cost for electing this feature, usually a reduced interest rate.

4. *Annuitization* – Every deferred annuity contract sold has a provision in it related to how the money accumulated in the annuity contract can be converted to a guaranteed stream of payments, including the timeframe and frequency of when the payments will be made. This process of converting the accumulated value of the annuity contract into a series of guaranteed periodic income payments is called annuitization. Annuity payments may only be made to the annuitant or to the annuitant and a surviving spouse in a joint-life arrangement. Annuitants can arrange for beneficiaries to receive a portion of the annuity balance upon their death.

    Here is how the process works. Upon receiving the lump sum of capital or premium, the life insurer makes calculations to determine the annuity payout. The key factors used in the calculation are the annuitant's current age, expected life span, payment option selected, and the projected interest rate the insurer will credit to the annuity balance. The resulting payout rate establishes the amount of income that the insurer will pay. So, it will have returned the entire annuity balance plus interest to the annuitant by the end of the payment period.

    The payment period may be a specified period (e.g., 5, 10, 15 or 20 years) called a period certain or the life expectancy of the purchaser. The significant difference between using a specified period versus a lifetime period is that, if the annuitant lives beyond their life expectancy, the life insurer must continue the payments until the annuitant's death. This is the insurance that the buyer is purchasing. The payments will continue for the annuitant's life and if that person lives very long and exhausts the premium paid for the contract, the life insurer must continue to pay the agreed-upon payment.

5. *Premium Payment Frequency* – Premiums for annuity products can be paid in two ways: by making a single premium or by flexible premium (making a number of payments). Single premium is just that – the buyer pays $75,000 once for the product. For flexible premium products, the buyer makes an initial deposit and has the option to make additional deposits on a regular or irregular basis. Flexible premium contracts may restrict the minimum size of additional payments to be made (e.g., a minimum of $500) and/or the amount of the initial premium paid to start the contract (e.g., $2,000).

6. *Minimum Premiums* – Annuity issuers establish the minimum premium to purchase their contracts. These minimum amounts vary by insurer and product type. Minimums can range from as little as $2,000 up to $100,000 depending on the type of annuity contract.

7. *Access to Cash* – When annuities were first brought to market, they only offered two ways to get access to cash from the contract. These were either on full surrender of the contract or via annuitization using one of the contractual-provided options. Over the years, the need to provide contract owners with more ways to get access to their cash without any surrender charges became increasingly important to potential buyers. Today's annuity products have limited liquidity but offer a number of

ways to get access to cash from an annuity contract. These include:

➤ *Free Partial Withdrawals* – This option allows the contract's owner to take up to a certain percentage (e.g., 10%) of the contract's value each year without surrender charges. Certain contracts allow the owner to accumulate free withdrawals not taken. For example, if the 10% free withdrawal was not taken for 3 years, 30% of the contract could be taken. Some carriers cap such a feature at a maximum 50% of the contract's value.

➤ *Systematic Withdrawals* – This option allows the contract's owner to request automatic withdrawals of a certain percentage of the annuity's value each year (e.g., 7%) until the contract value is reduced to zero.

➤ *Terminal Illness* – This option allows the contract owner to gain access, without incurring surrender charges, to most or all of the contract's value if he or she has been diagnosed with an illness that will result in their death within a certain timeframe, usually 2 years.

➤ *Nursing Home Confinement* – This option allows the contract owner to gain access, without incurring surrender charges, to most or all of the contract's value if he or she has been confined to a nursing home because of illness or incapacitation.

➤ *Long-Term Care* – This option allows the contract owner to gain access to the contract's value, without surrender charges, either in a lump sum or by requesting a monthly payout to pay the costs of a long-term care event.

➤ *Income Riders* – These riders, which are subject to an additional annual charge, trigger the payment of a certain percentage of the contract's value (e.g., 5%) for life. This payment stream can be stopped at any time and restarted by the contract holder and is different from annuitizing the contract in that it can be controlled by the owner.

Annuity contracts are not checking accounts. They are medium to long-term contracts but have limited access to liquidity available through the options described above.

OVERVIEW OF THE BUSINESS OF ANNUITIES

Industry Overview

Annuity products are created and sold by life insurance companies and are a major part of the U.S. life insurance industry. The U.S. life insurance business constitutes a large segment of the U.S. economy. As per the American Council of Life Insurers (ACLI) 2019 Life Insurers Fact Book (acli.com), the industry is made up of 773 companies, having almost $7 trillion of assets. These companies paid out $680 billion in benefits to policyholders in 2018. It is a huge industry. Of those 773 companies, the bulk of annuities are written by about 50 companies.

According to the Secure Retirement Institute's 2019 U.S. Individual Annuity Sales Survey, U.S. life insurance companies sold over $241 billion of annuity products. According to the survey, over 75% of sales were made by 20 companies.

Life insurance is also one of the most regulated businesses in the United States. Companies operate under a broad regulatory system that is overseen primarily by the states with certain federal requirements for certain of the products sold. Life insurers are regulated in all respects including what products they can sell, how they can invest policyholder funds, how much capital they must have in the business, and how they manage all risks in their business. As someone who ran companies in the U.S. for over two decades, I can tell you from personal experience, this regulatory system is robust and comprehensive. The industry operates to protect the policyholder.

Types of Life Insurance Companies

As per the ACLI's 2019 Life Insurers Fact Book, most life insurers are organized as either stock or mutual companies. Stock life insurance companies issue stock and are owned by their stockholders. These businesses can be privately held or traded on one of the major stock exchanges. Mutual companies are legally owned by their policyholders and, consequently, do not issue stock. According to ACLI, the majority of life insurers are stock companies — 580 or 75% of the industry. There were 109 mutual insurers and 84 fraternal and other companies. Fraternal benefit societies provide both social and insurance benefits to their members. These organizations are legally required to operate through a lodge system, allowing only lodge members and their families to own the fraternal society's insurance. Together, stock and mutual life insurers provide most of the insurance underwritten by U.S. organizations.

As of year-end 2018, the latest year available, the industry employed 2.7 million people. It had total assets of nearly $7 trillion and premium income of over $614 billion.

The ACLI discloses the following on its website that I think clearly summarizes the impact the U.S. life insurance industry has on the American economy:

"Life insurance is the cornerstone of financial security for millions of American families and businesses. It enables individuals and families from all economic brackets to maintain independence in the face of financial catastrophe. We believe America is strongest when its workers and families are able to save and plan for their financial futures. Savings in permanent life insurance and annuities alone represent more than 14 percent of Americans' long-term savings in this country. By providing tools for protection and savings, life insurance promotes personal responsibility and thus relieves pressure on government programs. 90 million American families depend on ACLI members for life insurance, annuities, retirement plans, long-term care insurance, disability income insurance, reinsurance, dental and vision and other supplemental benefits."

HOW ANNUITY COMPANIES ARE REGULATED

The U.S. life insurance industry is subject to substantial ongoing regulation for all aspects of its operations. In 1945, the Congress adopted the McCarran-Ferguson Act to declare that it would be in the public's best interest for states to regulate the business of insurance. This system of state regulation is still in effect today as the individual states license and regulate all of the 773 companies that sell life insurance. Each state names its department responsible for life insurers but they are normally found under titles of Department of Insurance, Financial Services Authority or Insurance Department. There is no federal government life insurance regulator or organization.

There is, however, a national organization that has been formed by all of the state regulators called the National Association of Insurance Commissioners (NAIC). The NAIC summarizes what it does in this quote taken directly from its website:

"The National Association of Insurance Commissioners (NAIC) is the U.S. standard-setting and regulatory support organization created and governed by the chief insurance regulators from the 50 states, the District of Columbia and five U.S. territories. Through the NAIC, state insurance regulators establish standards and best practices, conduct peer review, and coordinate their regulatory oversight. NAIC staff supports these efforts and represents the collective views of state regulators domestically and internationally. NAIC members, together with the central resources of the NAIC, form the national system of state-based insurance regulation in the U.S."

The organization's website (naic.org) contains numerous resources that can assist you in answering questions about regulation, individual companies, your state's insurance regulator, and insurance products.

State-Based Regulation

The individual states and their lawmakers create and approve laws to regulate insurance in their geography. They establish and fund the state insurance regulations; set up and name the regulatory bodies; and regularly review and revise state insurance laws. According to the NAIC – "The fundamental reason for government regulation of insurance is to protect American consumers. State systems are accessible and accountable to the public and sensitive to local social and economic conditions. State regulation has proven that it effectively protects consumers and ensures that promises made by insurers are kept."

The breadth, scope, and frequency of state-based insurance regulation is extensive and covers all areas of the operational and financial management of the companies. This system covers the following major areas: company licensing, producer licensing, product regulation, market conduct, financial regulation, and consumer services.

New Proposed Regulations of the Sales Process

As of mid-2020 when this book was being written, there is a significant amount of legislative and regulatory efforts being expended by the Securities and Exchange Commission (SEC), the Financial Institutions Regulatory Authority (FINRA), the Department of Labor (DOL), the National Association of Insurance Commissioners, and various state legislators to develop new standards on how annuities and investment products should be sold, disclosed, and presented. These efforts will likely result in new regulations regarding the disclosures, point-of-sale forms, required signatures, and the design and content of marketing materials used in the selling process. These changes are being made to improve consumer protections and disclosures. The proposed changes being deliberated do not fundamentally change how you should consider annuity products and how you use them as a tool to address financial risks.

This summarizes the nature and scope of how life insurers are regulated. If you have questions or need more in-depth information, contact your state's insurance department. Contact information can be found on the NAIC website for all states and territories.

SUMMARY

Annuity products in one contractual form or other have been with us for hundreds of years. Almost 199 million Americans already own one in the form of their future expected Social Security retirement benefit. The annuity industry and products are subject to heavy state-based regulation. The products' uses have been tested in numerous economic cycles and have proven financially strong and reliable. Lastly, these products have been designed to help individuals accumulate funds on a tax-advantaged basis to produce supplemental protected income in later life. The products have many core benefits for consumers.

CHAPTER 2

THE CORE BENEFITS OF ANNUITIES

INTRODUCTION

Annuity products are designed to offer core consumer benefits. Some of these benefits are included as an intrinsic part of the annuity contract without separate initial or ongoing charges. While other benefits, such as a Guaranteed Lifetime Withdrawal Benefit, come with a separate annual charge (e.g., 1%) that is paid from the annuity contract for as long as the benefit is elected by the consumer. Let's look at the major consumer benefits of annuity products.

UNLIMITED CONTRIBUTIONS FOR NON-QUALIFIED ANNUITIES

One of the biggest benefits annuities offer is that they allow you to put away cash and defer paying taxes. Unlike other tax-deferred retirement accounts such as 401(k)s and IRAs, there is no annual contribution limit for a non-qualified annuity. You can put as much money into these contracts as you deem prudent. Remember, never put all your eggs in one basket, and always diversify your savings choices. Unlimited contributions allow you to put away more money for retirement after you have maxed out other available options, such as 401(k)s, and is particularly useful for those that are closest to retirement age and who need to catch up.

TAX DEFERRAL

All the money you invest in annuity compounds, year after year, without any current tax bill from federal or state governments - that ability to keep every dollar invested, and working for you, can be a big advantage over taxable investments. Taxes become due on income earned by the annuity when they are withdrawn, which we discuss in Chapter 3.

PRINCIPAL PROTECTION

Fixed and fixed-indexed annuities pay a guaranteed minimum rate of return and guaranteed return of the principal deposited to buy the contract. The guarantees offered can range from a full return of principal to a return of over 80% of the deposit made. These contracts also provide a fixed series of payments under conditions determined when you buy the annuity.

Remember, during the fixed annuity's accumulation phase, the insurance company invests the premiums in high-quality, fixed-income investments like bonds. Because your rate of return is guaranteed, the insurance company bears all of the investment risk with fixed annuities.

ABILITY TO BE SWAPPED TAX FREE

The tax code allows one annuity contract to be swapped for another. This provision is called a Section 1035 Exchange. This exchange allows you to switch annuity contracts or companies while continuing to defer taxes, ensuring that your annuity stays up to date with the latest features and benefits and the best rates. You can stay with the same type of annuity or you could switch from one type of annuity to another if it would better meet your changing needs.

For example, let's say you invested in a variable annuity contract in 1995 when you were 35. At that time it made sense because variable annuities allowed you to participate in the equity market potential gains while deferring taxes. Now, imagine you just turn 60, and you are looking for the safety of principal protection and guarantees. A good choice might be a less risky and more guaranteed fixed annuity. You could exchange your variable annuity for a fixed annuity tax free. Since you've had your annuity for years, there would be no surrender charge. So, all of your money will go to work for you.

Another great use of Section 1035 is the ability to exchange life insurance contracts for annuity contracts. Many older people have paid-up, cash-value life insurance policies that they no longer need because they're retired, collecting a pension and Social Security, and have paid off their mortgage or are perhaps divorced, widowed, or no longer have any beneficiaries they are concerned for at their death. Section 1035 lets you exchange such a policy for an annuity, tax free. The owner, or owners, of the life insurance policy, and the new annuity, must be identical. A typical type of exchange is to swap a life insurance policy for an income annuity.

PROBATE AVOIDANCE

Most annuity contracts avoid the probate process as long as beneficiaries are properly designated. With annuities you can provide income for yourself during your retirement as well as for a beneficiary after your death. The typical annuity account will not go to probate because it has a named beneficiary. Assets with a named beneficiary, such as annuities and life insurance policies, typically bypass probate.

ACCESS TO CASH WHEN NEEDED

Annuity products, with the exception of certain immediate and deferred income annuities, are not designed to be liquid investments. They do, however, offer consumers a number of ways to access cash in case of an emergency. These include lump sum withdrawals, systematic withdrawals (e.g., 5% of the accumulated value each year), full contract surrenders, and use of the contract's annuitization options. As we will see in Chapter 3, withdrawals from an annuity contract can be subject to income taxes and, if made prior to age 59-and a-half, a penalty tax for early withdrawal.

OFFSET TO LONGEVITY RISK

Longevity risk is the risk of outliving your money. As we have discussed in the FinancialVerse books we are all living a lot longer. The question arises as to how we can accumulate enough assets to create an income to fund the living expenses for these extended years.

Annuities can help offset this risk by providing a guaranteed, protected, supplemental income stream during the retirement years. They can provide an income that is guaranteed for the rest of your life or for a period selected. An annuity can offer full or partial financial protection against longevity risk and can be a possible solution by providing predictable income payments in retirement.

GUARANTEED PROTECTED INCOME

All annuity contracts offer specific options to generate guaranteed protected income. This feature usually offers a number of options including lifetime, period certain (e.g., 10, 15 or 20-year durations) and survivorship. This is one of the core insurance benefits of annuity products.

DEATH BENEFITS

All deferred annuities provide for their remaining accumulated value to be paid quickly following the owner's passing to whomever they have designated as the beneficiaries, typically bypassing the delays and expenses of the probate process as stated above. Some annuities further offer guaranteed minimum death benefits - often available for an additional annual charge that is deducted from the annuity's value, which can provide for a death benefit that exceeds the annuity's accumulated value. Most all deferred annuity contracts pay a death benefit equal to the accumulated value of the annuity contract. A minority of contracts charge a fee or surrender charge if the annuitant dies within certain designated time periods.

Income annuities offer options that will pay to designated beneficiaries the full or partial amount of unpaid benefits upon death of the contract's annuitant.

NURSING HOME, LONG-TERM CARE AND
TERMINAL ILLNESS BENEFITS

Most of today's deferred annuity products allow the contract owner to withdraw, without any fees or charges, the accumulated value of the annuity contract if they are admitted to a nursing home, are diagnosed with a terminal illness and have less than 12 months to live or have a qualifying long-term care event. Annuity contracts specify how these benefits are triggered, the documentation needed to support the event, any waiting periods, and how the payments will be made.

In the last few years many insurance carriers have added, for a fee, benefits that include additional income or expense reimbursement for long-term care events. Many of these benefits come with a separate charge.

SUMMARY

Annuity contracts offer a multitude of consumer benefits. In recent years the number of such benefits have increased with new long-term care benefits added to the suite of available benefits.

CHAPTER 3

ANNUITY INCOME TAX BENEFITS AND NEGATIVES

CONGRESS AND THE LAW

Congress has written laws as part of the Internal Revenue Code that pertain to the tax aspects of annuity products. It is not required for you, as a potential buyer, to have in-depth knowledge of the ins and outs of the entire U.S. tax code. There are income, estate, and other tax considerations for these products. A financial advisor, tax professional, or attorney can help you navigate the details, and determine exactly what is and is not taxable. What I will do in this section is to give you an overview of the key tax aspects of annuities.

TAXATION BASICS FOR ANNUITY PRODUCTS

In this section we will focus on the major matters to allow you to gain a general working understanding of the tax aspects of these products. This section does not address all of the taxation aspects of annuity products. Please consult a financial professional or your tax advisor for specific information about tax questions. Do not act and make decisions without consulting these professionals.

Here are the major tax aspects of annuity products. I present them in a question-and-answer format to make them easier to understand and to fully cover the basic issues.

Are Annuity Premiums Tax Deductible?

For a non-qualified annuity, premiums are paid with after-tax monies and are not tax deductible. At the same time, there is no limit to the amount of money that can be contributed to non-qualified annuities.

Premiums paid for a qualified or IRA annuity may be deductible in whole, or in part, based on the annual limitations and income of the taxpayer.

Is Income Earned by An Annuity Subject to Current Taxation?

No. Interest, dividends, capital gains, and other income credited to an annuity are not taxed until they are withdrawn. This "deferral of current taxation" is one of the major benefits of annuity products. In other words, earnings are tax deferred and reinvested to help accumulate assets for retirement. Congress designed this to help Americans accumulate more money for their later years. As a result, money may be transferred from one investment option to another inside an annuity without triggering a tax liability. This is not true for stocks, bonds, and taxable mutual fund investments. For these investments, transferring amounts from one investment to another will be treated as a sale and any gains will be taxable.

The one major exception to the rule of no current taxation is if a deferred annuity contract is not owned by an individual but rather by an entity such as a corporation. In this situation, the contract is not eligible for tax deferral, in most cases. Rather, the entity is taxed each year on the increase in the net surrender value of the contract, minus premiums paid during the year. Congress enacted this requirement to ensure that the tax deferral granted by annuities is used primarily as a vehicle for individuals' retirement savings.

One of the major negatives of annuity products is that income from an annuity product is taxed at ordinary income tax rates and is not eligible for taxation at capital gains rates. Again, this was done purposefully by Congress as part of granting deferral from current taxation for annuity products.

One other consideration relating to income taken/withdrawn from annuity contracts is that, starting in 2013, distributions from non-qualified annuity contracts is generally subject to the 3.8% Medicare tax on investment income for taxpayers with adjusted gross income (with certain modifications), over $250,000 in the case of married couples, filing jointly and qualifying widow(er)s with dependent children, $125,000 in the case of married taxpayers filing separately, or $200,000 in the case of other taxpayers.

How Are Annuity Withdrawals Taxed?

How withdrawals are taxed, and the amount subject to taxation, depends on the type of withdrawal taken from an annuity contract. Let's go through the major types of annuity withdrawals and how each is taxed.

Complete Surrenders

When an owner fully surrenders or cashes in 100% of an annuity contract, the excess of the amount received over the owner's investment in the contract is taxable. Generally, the investment in the contract is the amount of premiums paid (less any principal that has been previously returned to the contract owner without tax) at the time of distribution. For example, John owns a fixed annuity he purchased in 2014 for $15,000 that now has an accumulated value of $25,000. He decides to surrender the contract. He will pay tax on the $10,000 gain at ordinary income tax rates.

Pre-Age 59½ Distributions

Deferred annuities were created to be long-term retirement savings vehicles by Congress and granted the tax-deferral incentive. To protect against taxpayers abusing this incentive, Congress mandated that withdrawals made before age 59½ from deferred annuities may be subject to a 10% federal tax penalty on the taxable amount of earnings withdrawn in addition to any income taxes due on that amount. (Please note that there are exceptions to this rule that do not trigger the 10% tax, like the death or disability of the contract owner.)

Partial Surrenders

A partial surrender from a qualified annuity contract, is fully taxable to the extent of the amount received. When a contract owner receives a partial surrender of money from a non-qualified annuity, distributions received that are less than what the contract has earned on a cumulative basis are subject to taxation at the owner's ordinary income tax rate. As discussed below, however, non-qualified annuity income payments elected under what is called a payout or settlement option in the annuity contract receive more favorable tax treatment than partial surrenders.

When calculating taxation for non-qualified annuity contracts, the tax rule on withdrawals is "interest and earnings first" or the "last in first out" (LIFO) rule. Under this rule, interest and earnings are considered withdrawn first for federal income tax purposes. For example, if someone invested $25,000 in a fixed indexed annuity and the contract is now worth $40,000, the first $15,000 withdrawn is considered to be interest earned and is taxable as ordinary income. The remaining $25,000 is not taxed because it is considered a return of principal. Withdrawals are taxed until all interest and earnings are withdrawn; the principal then can be withdrawn without tax.

The LIFO rule is intended to encourage the use of annuities for long-term savings and retirement. Congress decided that the advantage of tax deferral should not be accompanied by the ability to withdraw principal first with no tax payable until all principal is withdrawn. Different rules apply to tax-qualified annuities (such as IRAs), under which withdrawals are taxed on a pro rata basis to the extent there were any after-tax contributions made to the contract.

Annuity Payouts Under a Payout or Settlement Option

All payouts received from a qualified annuity contract are usually taxable. Different rules apply to tax-qualified annuities (such as IRAs) when after-tax contributions have also been made. In these situations, withdrawals are taxed on a pro rata basis to the extent there were any after-tax contributions made to the contract.

Minimum Required Distributions at Age 72

Congress has mandated that certain minimum required distributions begin at age 72 from qualified annuity contracts. According to irs.gov, required minimum distributions (RMDs), generally, are minimum amounts that a retirement plan account owner must withdraw annually starting with the year that he or she reaches 72 (70½, if you reached that age before January 1, 2020), if later, the year in which he or she retires. However, if the retirement plan account is an IRA or the account owner is a 5% owner of the business sponsoring the retirement plan, the RMDs must begin once the account holder is age 72 (70½ if you reached that age before January 1, 2020), regardless of whether he or she is retired.

The minimum required distribution provision exists to ensure that tax deferral does not go on forever, and that taxes are eventually paid on the amounts saved. However, a key point to remember is that, unlike qualified plans, there are no minimum required distribution payments for non-qualified annuities. Distributions from non-qualified annuity contracts are at the discretion of the contract owner.

Annuitization

Non-qualified annuity contract owners can elect a number of payout or settlement options based on what is offered as part of the annuity contract they have purchased. The basic rule for non-qualified annuity payouts or settlement options (as distinguished from withdrawals) is that the money a contract owner invests in the contract, returns in equal tax-free installments over the payment period. The remainder of the amount received each year is treated as the earnings on the owner's premiums and is included in the income. The income portion is taxed at ordinary income tax rates, not capital gains rates. The total amount that is received tax free can never exceed the premiums the owner paid for the contract. This ratio of return of the investment made in the contract to the amount withdrawn is called the exclusion ratio. This is fully explained below.

The taxable portion of each payment is equal to the excess of the payment over the "exclusion amount." With a fixed annuity, the exclusion amount generally is computed by (a) dividing the premiums paid for the annuity by the total expected return from all scheduled annuity payments, and (b) multiplying each payment by this "exclusion ratio." With a variable annuity, because the expected return cannot be predicted, the exclusion amount is generally computed by dividing the premiums paid for the contract, by the number of years that payments are expected to be made. For a lifetime annuity, the expected return is always computed by reference to the annuitant's life expectancy as determined using IRS tables.

To illustrate, assume that a male age 65 elects a lifetime annuity and his investment in the contract is $100,000. Assume further that he has elected to receive annual variable annuity payments, and the payment for the first year is $8,000. Since the payments are variable, they will vary each year thereafter. (For simplicity, this illustration assumes annual annuity payments, although monthly or quarterly payments are more common.) Applicable IRS tables indicate that such a person aged 65 is expected to live 20 years. The portion of each annuity payment excluded from income is $5,000, which is $100,000 divided by 20. During the first year, $5,000 of the $8,000 will be excluded from income, and $3,000 will be included as taxable. The $5,000 is excluded each year until the total investment in the contract has been received.

Partial Annuitizations

In some cases, the owner of a deferred annuity contract may wish to apply only a portion of the contract's cash value (rather than the entire cash value) to produce a series of annuity payments under the contract, while leaving the contract's remaining cash value in the deferral or accumulation stage. For example, the owner's current financial need may be for annuity payments that are less than the payments the contract's full cash value would produce, or the owner may wish to "ladder" or "stagger" annuity payments to take advantage of future changes in annuity purchase rates. Prior to 2011, there was no specific rule in the tax code regarding such "partial annuitizations." Starting in 2011, however, the tax code provides that partial annuitizations of non-qualified annuities are treated the same as other annuitizations, as long as the resulting annuity payments are made for a period of at least 10 years, or over the life, or lives, of one or more individuals. In such cases, the annuitized and non-annuitized portions of the contract are treated as separate contracts and the after-tax investment in the contract is allocated pro rata between them for purposes of applying the rules governing the taxation of distributions.

Payouts from Living Benefit Riders

Income received by the contract owner by electing a living benefit rider is taxed as ordinary income to the extent there is a gain in the contract.

How Are Annuities Taxed on Death of the Contract Owner?

When an owner of an annuity dies, the general rule is that certain distributions must be made. The tax policy behind this rule is to prevent the prolonged deferral of income tax on the gains in an annuity contract that would occur if ownership could be passed from person to person without taxation occurring.

If an owner dies on, or after, the annuity payments have begun, but before the entire interest in the contract has been distributed (e.g., if the owner dies 5 years into a 10-year-guaranteed payout term), the remaining portion must be distributed at least as rapidly as under the method of distribution in effect at the time of death.

If an owner dies before the annuity payments begin, the general rule is that the entire interest in the contract must be distributed within 5 years after the date of the owner's death. Under this rule, a beneficiary has the following choices:

➤ Take the total amount due under the contract and pay taxes at that time (a full surrender of the contract now).

➤ Make withdrawals over the course of the next 5 years and pay taxes on each withdrawal, with the remainder of the contract value growing tax deferred (the 5-year option).

➤ Wait up to 5 years with the contract value growing tax deferred, then surrender the contract and pay the taxes due (full surrender after 5 years).

An exception to the 5-year rule described above is available for cases in which payments are made to a beneficiary over their life expectancy. Specifically, within 12 months of the owner's death, a beneficiary can (a) annuitize the remaining interest over his or her life expectancy, and receive the favorable tax treatment accompanying annuity payments, or (b) begin withdrawals over a period not exceeding the beneficiary's life expectancy, calculated in a manner specified in IRS rules, and pay taxes on each withdrawal on an income-first basis.

There is a special provision if the beneficiary of the annuity is the contract owner's spouse. In this case, for purposes after-death distribution rules, if an individual is the owner under a contract and the spouse is the beneficiary, then following the owner's death the surviving spouse is treated as the "owner" of the contract. In such cases, the after-death distribution rules take effect upon the surviving spouse's death rather than upon the original owner's death. This means that the surviving spouse can assume ownership of the annuity and continue the contract's provisions as if no change in ownership had taken place.

Can I Exchange One Annuity Contract for Another Annuity or a Life Insurance Contract?

An annuity contract can be exchanged for another annuity contract but not for a life insurance contract. Section 1035 of the Internal Revenue Code lays down the rules governing these types of transactions. Making an exchange of annuity contracts may allow the contract owner to take advantage of new features and benefits from the new contract, that did not exist at the time of purchase of the old contract.

When a contract owner purchases a new annuity contract to replace an existing one, the new contract is referred to as a replacement contract. Replacement contracts usually occur in connection with a tax-free exchange of non-qualified contracts under Section 1035 of the Internal Revenue Code or because of a rollover or direct transfer of a qualified plan contract (e.g., an individual retirement annuity) from one life insurance company to another. Annuity owners, generally, can exchange their annuity contracts for new ones, tax free. In both qualified plans, and non-qualified annuities, depending upon the terms of the contract, it may also be possible to transfer, tax free, a portion of the contract to a new contract issued by the same or a different carrier, while continuing the remaining portion of the contract from which the partial transfer was taken. Special rules must be followed to assure that either a complete or a partial exchange or transfer qualifies for tax-free treatment.

The reasons for an exchange of annuity contracts can include:

- The owner has a fixed annuity with a substantially lower interest rate than other contracts currently available.

- The company that issued the current contract is not as financially strong as it was in the past.

- The new contract may have better features, such as an enhanced death benefit, income benefits, long-term care provisions, portfolio rebalancing, or dollar cost averaging.

- The new contract may have more or better-performing investment options.

- The new contract may have lower fees and charges.

➤ Many states have passed regulations requiring certain procedures be followed before an annuity contract is replaced. The contract purchaser and the agent must sign a statement as to whether the contract being purchased will replace an existing one. If so, the new insurance company must promptly notify the old insurance company. The new insurance company must provide the purchaser with a prescribed statement about important factors to consider before buying the replacement contract. In some cases, a surrender charge may be incurred by exchanging the old contract and a new surrender charge period may start on the new contract. For this reason, an individual and his, or her, financial advisor should carefully evaluate a proposed exchange to ensure that it is in the contract owner's best interest. States have adopted replacement regulations ensuring full disclosure in these situations and affording other protections. States also may provide longer free-look periods for replacement contracts than for other annuity contracts.

Can I Pay My Long-term Care Insurance Benefits from My Annuity Contract?

Yes, you can pay long-term care premiums using your non-qualified annuity contract without paying income tax on any amounts used to pay the premiums provided your contract allows such withdrawals. The Pension Protection Act of 2006 provided that all distributions from non-qualified annuities, for qualified long-term care expenses, are tax-free, effective 2010, regardless of cost basis, whether the distributions are from the cash value component of your annuity or from your annuity's long-term care extension of benefits provision. These income tax-free withdrawals allow you to protect your retirement by guaranteeing that you have funds available for long-term care expenses.

SUMMARY

Congress granted significant tax benefits to annuity products including the deferral of taxes on current earnings from the contract. In exchange for these tax advantages, certain restrictions on the timing, amount, and taxation of distributions were put in place. When purchasing or withdrawing funds from an annuity contract, please consult a professional to fully understand the tax ramifications of your action, prior to taking it.

CHAPTER 4

ANNUITY PRODUCT TYPES

THE SIX MAJOR PRODUCT TYPES

There are six major types of annuities—fixed annuities, variable annuities, buffered or structured annuities, fixed indexed annuities, immediate income annuities, and deferred income annuities. All product types, except for immediate income and deferred income annuities, can be purchased with either a single premium payment (e.g., $25,000) or by making a number of premium payments (e.g., $5,000 per year for 6 years or $1,000 per month). The latter is called a flexible payment schedule with the consumer making various payments in varying amounts as they desire. Life insurers specify what minimum premiums are required for each product they sell. Both types of income annuities are usually purchased with a single premium payment.

There are a number of different product designs for each product type. The proper type of annuity contract, and what is best for you, depends on several variables, including your age, risk tolerance, need for access to cash in case of an emergency, fees you are willing to pay, income goals, and when you want to begin receiving annuity income (e.g., now, at retirement, or at much older ages – say age 85).

For your particular situation, each type of annuity product has positives and negatives. In Chapter 6 we discuss these in detail. As a potential annuity buyer, it is important that you have a basic understanding of the different types of annuities so that you can make the right decision. It is best to work with a financial professional to determine which type of annuity fits your particular needs for the financial risks you are looking to mitigate.

Let's look at the six major annuity product types. Fixed, variable, buffered, and fixed-indexed products possess the key characteristics of an annuity described in Chapter 1. Immediate and deferred income annuities share common characteristics with the exception of when their payments begin.

FIXED ANNUITIES

Fixed annuities earn a guaranteed rate of interest. All investments supporting this contract are managed by the issuing life insurance company. Fixed annuity contracts earn interest at a rate that has historically been higher than bank products, such as certificates of deposit. With fixed annuity contracts you have the option to defer income or draw income immediately. These contracts are popular among retirees and pre-retirees who want a no-cost, principal protected, and guaranteed fixed return.

Multi-year guarantee fixed annuities, or MYGAs, is a term used to describe a fixed annuity that has an interest rate guarantee for the same period of time as its surrender period. For example, an annuity with a guaranteed interest rate of 3% per year for 5 years, and surrender charges that last for 5 years, after which there are no surrender penalties, is a MYGA. Some MYGAs offer a higher or bonus interest rate the first year, and a lower, but guaranteed rate, for all subsequent years of the surrender period – e.g., 4.5% first year, with a guaranteed renewal at 3% for years 2-5. When considering these contracts, you need to calculate and understand what the contract's return will be for the entire 5-year period.

VARIABLE ANNUITIES

Variable annuities are so named because their earnings and income payments fluctuate with the performance of specific investment funds that the contract owner designates for their premiums. All decisions about how the money in the variable annuity contract is invested are made by the contract owner from investment funds offered by the life insurer. These investments are made available to the contract owner by offering what are called subaccounts (equity, bond, and some fixed-return mutual funds). The contract's value is determined by the performance of the subaccounts. As this product offers investment subaccounts that are securities and could lose money, the financial professional selling you this product must have a securities license in addition to their license to sell annuity products.

Available Additional Variable Annuity Riders

In order to make variable annuities more appealing and less risky to consumers, life insurers usually offer a range of optional riders that can be added to the variable annuity contract for an additional charge. These riders include guaranteed minimum death benefits to provide a legacy for your heirs, guaranteed minimum accumulation benefits that guarantee a minimum rate of growth (often as high as 5% annually), and lifetime income benefits that guarantee you a regular monthly, quarterly, or annual payment for your lifetime, even if your account balance goes to zero.

Key Additional Features

Variable annuities also offer a number of key features that include:

Death Benefits

A basic insurance feature of most variable annuities is death benefits. Death benefits are designed to insure and preserve your investment for the purpose of passing on to heirs. There are different types of variable annuity death benefits, but typically they ensure that when you die, your heirs will receive at least as much money as you invested into the annuity, less any withdrawals you took from your account (even if the value of the annuity contract has declined). Death benefits are a popular way of providing variable annuity buyers with the peace of mind that regardless of market performance, their heirs will receive at least the initial investment.

Living Benefits

Another key feature of most variable annuities is what are called living benefits. Just as death benefits insure an investment payout for their heirs, living benefits insure payout of the investment for their own use, should the account value decline significantly, or that withdrawals can be taken over a lifetime. For example, currently one of the most popular types of living benefits is a lifetime withdrawal benefit, which guarantees a stream of income that cannot be outlived while still allowing access to the contract's principal, if needed. Living benefits are available for an additional annual charge that ranges between .7% and 1.25%.

Surrender Charges

As we have discussed previously, most deferred annuities come with a surrender period of 5 to 7 years. This is a period during which the insurance company expects you will let your money grow and not make significant withdrawals. Most annuity contracts will allow you to take out 10% per year in withdrawals without incurring a surrender charge. Surrender penalties decrease over time. For example, an annuity with a standard 7-year surrender period may impose a fee of 8% on withdrawals made in the first year, but only 1% for withdrawals made in the 7th year. Note that the 10% annual penalty-free withdrawal is typical of most annuities, but not all.

Variable Annuity Fees and Expenses

There are essentially five types of fees you should be aware of when investing in a variable annuity: investment fees for each subaccount you put money into; surrender charges should you withdraw funds early; the annual fees for any optional riders; penalties imposed by the IRS if you withdraw funds prior to the age of 59½; and mortality, expense and administrative fees (ME&A fees). Yes, variable annuities come with lots of fees that you will need to understand while purchasing the product. ME&A fees are confusing to many people and you need to understand what they are for. Just as you pay an annual fee for your auto insurance or homeowner's insurance, base variable annuity contracts have an annual fee, called mortality, expense and administrative fees or ME&A fees. The industry average for ME&A fees is about 1.25%, whereas 1.65% is high and anything below 1% is considered to be low. The industry average for administrative fees is 0.15%. In sum, ME&A fees vary depending on the contract and features but should not exceed 2% of the account value (and are often far less).

Contract Maintenance Charges

Insurance carriers usually charge a flat fee for each variable annuity contract per year. The industry average is $35. Typically the maintenance charges are waived on accounts above a certain size (e.g., $50,000).

The Four Basic Types of Variable Annuity Contracts

When choosing a base variable annuity contract, each insurance company typically allows you to choose between one and four different versions of their product. The four that you will normally encounter include:

➤ Core – This product comes with the company's standard surrender period, usually about seven years.

➤ No Surrender Charges – This product has no surrender period and, hence, no withdrawal penalties. However, the annual fees are typically higher in exchange for having no surrender charges.

➤ Short Surrender Period – These products have a short surrender period, usually three or four years. But they also typically have higher annual fees and lower guaranteed returns.

➤ Bonus Contract – A bonus annuity adds an additional percentage to your premium, usually in the first year (often as high as 5%, so if you invest $100,000, you would receive an additional $5,000 credited to your account). These bonuses usually come with restrictions on how they vest and can be withdrawn.

BUFFERED OR STRUCTURED ANNUITIES

Introduced in 2010, buffered annuities (also referred to as variable indexed annuities, indexed-linked variable annuities, structured annuities or registered-index linked annuities) are a category of variable annuity products that is seeing a significant increase in sales according to the Secure Retirement Institute. I like the term buffered used to describe them because this product buffers the loss the policyholder incurs if the investments underlying the annuity lose money. In reality, these products have a mix of the characteristics of fixed indexed annuities and variable annuities. From a regulatory standpoint they are insurance products with an investment element and, as such, can only be sold by licensed insurance professionals who can also sell investment products. As you learn more about these products, you will see why I highlight these products as a separate product type because of their increasing popularity and rapid sales growth.

Comparison to Other Annuities

How do buffered annuities compare to other annuities? First, they are similar to fixed indexed annuities as the products' interest earned is tied to a particular index, such as the S&P 500 or the MSCI EAFE. Buffered annuities, however, allow the policyholder to capture much more of the upside of the index than a fixed indexed annuity, but not all of the equity market increase like a variable annuity does. Unlike a fixed indexed annuity, a buffered annuity merely protects some of the downside, and can cause a policyholder to lose money, similar to a variable annuity. The ability to lose money is why this product is considered an investment that requires a securities license to sell.

The Product's Mechanics

When you purchase a buffered annuity, you normally select the length of the index term you want (usually 1, 3, or 6 years); what index offered by the life insurer that you would like to participate in; how much protection from loss you desire; and the interest crediting method. These products offer a number of differing indices and crediting methods (e.g., caps/participation, spreads, and triggers). The upside and downside limits of buffered annuities are connected. So, a higher level of protection from the downside risk of loss means a lower cap on upside potential, and vice versa. When the underlying index performance is positive during a term, your annuity may earn interest credits limited by a cap or participation rate. Index declines can result in negative interest credits, mitigated by the level of protection you have chosen from any loss.

The Key Product Choice – How Much Downside Protection You Want

A "buffer" or a "floor" are two options that insurance carriers offer to limit exposure to market losses for these products. A buffer is the percentage of downside protection, typically 10, 20 or 30%. For example, if the index you have selected declines 15% and you choose a 10% buffer (loss to be absorbed by the insurance carrier), you would incur a loss of 5%. If you select a 30% buffer, losses up to that amount are absorbed by the life insurance company. In exchange for higher buffer percentages, you get lower participation in the index you have selected. A floor design is the opposite of the buffer option. In this case, you would be exposed to the percentage loss up to the floor amount, but you are protected against any loss after this percentage. For example, if you choose a product with a 10% "floor" and the market declines 15%, you would lose 10%, because the floor limits the downside.

Buffered annuities have the standard characteristics of all annuity products such as tax deferral, annuitization options, and death benefits equal to accumulated values but usually do not offer living benefits such as lifetime minimum withdrawals. Industry experts often say that this product category is for the variable annuity customer who wants to get protection from major potential losses.

Why Buy A Buffered Product?

Buffered annuities are typically designed to help you accumulate money for retirement or other long-term needs. They protect you against major market losses thereby protecting your principal. If you are searching for an annuity option that provides lifetime income, a different annuity solution may be a better fit. These products appeal to consumers who would like to take more risk than a fixed indexed annuity but would like some protection from equity market losses. To obtain this protection/return mix, the consumer gives up the ability to receive full equity market upside returns.

FIXED INDEXED ANNUITIES

A fixed indexed annuity (also known as an equity indexed annuity) is a type of fixed annuity that grows at a rate greater than of, a) an annual, guaranteed minimum rate of return; or b) the return from a specified stock market index (such as the S&P 500), reduced by certain expenses and carrier mandated limitations. This type of annuity has grown in popularity in the past decade. The guaranteed minimum return differentiates the fixed indexed annuity contract from a variable annuity, which does not have such a minimum and where, in fact, you can lose money.

Fixed index annuities offer the ability to participate in some of the gains associated with a rising stock market while at the same time having strong contractual minimums. These contracts do not produce equity market returns and should be purchased with the understanding that they should produce returns greater that a pure fixed annuity but substantially less than equity market returns.

Fixed index annuity interest is calculated using a formula that determines how much of the percentage change in the index applies to the account value of the fixed indexed annuity. Insurers use a variety of calculation methodologies for these formulas including those involving participation rates, caps, and spreads, to limit the amount of interest that can be credited based on the change in value of the underlying stock market index. It is critical that the consumer fully understand how interest will be earned and credited to their fixed index annuity contract as part of the purchase process.

Here is an example of how interest is calculated for a contract that has a participation rate formula tied to the S&P 500 index under two scenarios. For the first scenario, if the FIA has a participation rate of 30% of the change in the value of the S&P 500 index, and that index returns 10% in a policy year, 3% is credited to the annuity contract (10% x .3). In the second scenario, if the index loses 28% for the year, the minimum interest for the contract will be 0%. This is the key benefit of indexed products–you get reduced upside earning potential in exchange for downside or loss protection if the index declines. If you had your money invested in the equity markets, you would have lost 28% in that year.

These contracts appeal to retirees and pre-retirees who want to conservatively participate in potential market appreciation with downside principal protection.

IMMEDIATE INCOME ANNUITIES

An immediate income annuity guarantees payments, which can start right away, for a period of time (called a period certain) or for the annuitant's life. The payments made can be fixed (e.g., $600 per month) or variable (increasing 3% per year) based on the consumer's selection.

Here is how they work. In exchange for a lump sum premium, the life insurer guarantees to make regular income payments until death, or for a specified period of time, typically starting 1 to 12 months after receipt of the premium. Immediate annuity payments are typically higher than other annuities because they include a return of the buyer's principal, as well as interest, and also offer favorable tax treatment. In almost every case, once a consumer purchases an immediate income annuity, it is an irrevocable decision between the purchaser and the insurance company and cannot be voided. If the immediate income annuity was purchased with after-tax dollars, each payment received will be part return of principal and part interest. So, a portion of each payment will not be taxable. The percentage that is not taxable is called the exclusion ratio.

These are popular among retirees and pre-retirees who use the payments to supplement their income and are comfortable sacrificing principal in exchange for guaranteed income.

Types of Immediate Income Annuities

These are the key types of immediate income annuities:

- ➤ Fixed Income Annuities – Most immediate annuities are fixed income annuities. They pay a set amount for life and do not vary.

- ➤ Fixed Income Annuities with An Increasing Payment Percentage – These are fixed immediate income annuities where the payments increase by a contractually agreed percentage each year, say 2%. In exchange for increasing payments, the buyer receives a lower starting payment. This type of product is used by individuals who want some protection against inflation risk and believe they have a good chance of a long-life expectancy.

➤ Immediate Variable Income Annuities – These contracts may pay more than a fixed income annuity, as the contract is invested in equity market related investments. If the stock market performs better than fixed interest rates over the life of the investment, the payments from this contract could exceed those from a fixed contract. On the downside, payments will vary and could fare worse over time.

DEFERRED INCOME ANNUITIES AND QLACS

A deferred income annuity (DIA), is an annuity contract between you and a life insurance company. You make a lump sum payment to the insurance company in exchange for guaranteed lifetime income that begins at a future date, up to 40 years later in some cases. These products are sometimes referred to as "longevity annuities" because the income stream can be triggered so far in the future. Many people use them to protect against running out of income should they have very long lifespans. Deferred income annuities work similarly to immediate annuities, except that the payments don't start immediately.

With deferred income annuities, you shift the risk of outliving your income to the insurer, who promises to pay you a certain amount of income for the rest of your life beginning at the age you elect. The insurer also assumes your interest and market risk; even if the market and interest rates go down significantly during your deferral period, you still get the same guaranteed payment amount. In short, the investment risk and the interest rate risk during the deferral period are assumed by the issuing life insurance company.

In exchange for assuming these risks, deferred income annuity contracts are irrevocable, meaning they have no cash surrender value and no cash withdrawals are permitted. Their purpose is to provide income in later life to protect against longevity risk. Effectively you are granted a guaranteed income payment in the future if you live that long.

As with all fixed immediate annuities, the rise and fall of the stock market or interest rates does not affect the amount of future income you will receive from your deferred income annuity. When you sign the contract, you decide when you want to start receiving income and the insurance company will guarantee you a set income. Most deferred income annuities allow for subsequent contributions to your contract, but the way these subsequent deposits are factored into future income varies from one product to another. It often depends on the frequency of the subsequent contributions.

It cannot be stressed enough that deferred income annuities are not liquid, and you have little to no ability to get access to the cash you invested in the contract. When you invest in a deferred income annuity, you completely forfeit the initial premium in exchange for the insurance company's promise to pay you in the future. There are several products that have some liquidity options; however, they can be difficult to invoke and are often subject to surrender fees.

Higher Payouts Than Immediate Annuities

Deferred income annuities offer significantly higher payouts than immediate income annuities because the income payments start much later in life. For example, let's take a hypothetical 60-year-old considering an investment in a deferred income annuity versus an immediate annuity:

Daniel is 63 years old, nearing retirement, and expects to follow in his parents' footsteps and live into his late 80s. He decides to invest $100,000 in a deferred income annuity, and he wants the payments to start at age 85. At the time of this writing, after the 20-year deferral period, Daniel will be able to withdraw around $28,000 per year for the rest of his life. So, if he lives to age 95, he will have received $280,000 in income from his initial $100,000 investment!

Now, what if Daniel decided instead to wait until he is 80 years old and invest in an immediate annuity? Let's assume that the $100,000 he had at age 60 was invested in conservative investments yielding 3% interest per year for that 20 years. So, by age 80 he had about $180,000. At the time of this writing, an 80-year-old investing $180,000 will receive about $1,400 per month, or about $16,800 per year, from an immediate annuity. So, if he lives to age 95, he will have received about $252,000 in income.

Optional Contractual Benefits

With most deferred income annuity products, as we have noted, you forfeit the principal in exchange for the guarantee of future payments. In order to pass on your investment to your heirs in the event of your death, some insurance companies offer optional riders that can be added to a deferred income annuity. These include:

> The ability to pass on your investment to your designated beneficiary when you die – depending on the annuity, either return of your initial premium or your remaining income stream.

> Some insurance companies also offer optional benefits that increase your guaranteed income, at a fixed or variable rate, to hedge against the effects of inflation.

> Some deferred income annuities only offer a stream of income that is guaranteed for life. Others may offer different and more flexible payout options, such as joint life, a period certain

guarantee, or a period certain guarantee with cash refund. With a joint-life option, payments are guaranteed for your lifetime, or the lifetime of the joint-life annuitant, whichever is longer. With a period certain guarantee, your payments are guaranteed to you for a set length of time, or your heirs, should you pass during the guaranteed period. Lastly, a period certain with cash refund option guarantees you a stream of income for a set length of time. Should you pass away during that time, the sum of the payments for the rest of the period would be given to your heirs upon your death.

These various options come at an additional fee, which reduces the income payments, so be sure to review them with a financial adviser that specializes in annuities.

Deferred income annuity products appeal to people who want guaranteed income in the future, not now, or who want to create a ladder of income over different periods later in life. For example, they may want to work in retirement but know that they will eventually stop working and, at that point, and not before, will need guaranteed income from an annuity.

QLACs – A Special Type of Deferred Income Annuity

Beginning at age 72, owners with assets in qualified accounts (e.g., IRAs and 401(k)s) are mandated to take what are called required minimum distributions (RMDs). If RMDs are not taken as prescribed, the taxpayer can be subject to significant tax penalties. These withdrawals are taxed as ordinary income. Some investors, however, may not want to take RMDs on their entire pre-tax account balance at age 72, as it would provide them with more income than they need and they want to take the distributions later in their lives to protect against running out of money. They do this so they have money to cover basic living expenses that may also increase as they age, such as pre-scription drugs, in-home care, and other healthcare expenses.

A QLAC is a deferred income annuity that allows withdrawals from certain types of qualified accounts to begin beyond age 72 without conflicting with RMD rules. QLACs provide the owner with flexibility to defer the income start date until age 85. They can only be funded, however, with assets from a Traditional IRA or with assets from an eligible employer-sponsored qualified plan including a 401(k), 403(b), or governmental 457(b).

Similar to other deferred income annuity contracts, QLACs are irrevocable, have no cash surrender value, and no withdrawals are permitted. Their purpose is to provide income in later life to protect against longevity risk.

These products are designed and have been approved by the Internal Revenue Service to offset the risks of aging. It is important to understand that the IRS has placed limits on how much money can be invested in QLACs, and you are ultimately responsible for ensuring that you meet applicable rules. These limits change periodically. So, you should check the current status. And like RMDs, there are substantial penalties for failing to follow the limits outlined below.

The premium amount you deposit into a QLAC is subject to two limitations:

1. Total sum of QLAC premiums cannot exceed $135,000 regard-less of funding source; and

2. QLAC premiums from a given funding source cannot exceed 25% of that funding source's value.

The $135,000 QLAC limit for 2020 applies to individual taxpayers with $540,000, or more, in eligible accounts. If you have less than $540,000, you can't use more than 25% of those assets to buy a QLAC. This is calculated based on the sum of your eligible balances as of December 31 of the previous year. If you have $540,000 or more in those assets, you can use up to $135,000 to buy a QLAC (IRS Notice 2019-59).

SUMMARY

There are six major types of annuities: fixed annuities, variable annuities, buffered or structured, fixed indexed annuities, immediate income annuities, and deferred income annuities. There are a number of different product designs for each product type. The proper type of annuity contract and what is best for you depends on several variables, including your age, risk tolerance, need for access to cash in case of an emergency, fees you are willing to pay, income goals, and when you want to begin receiving annuity income (e.g., now, at retirement, or much later in life, say after age 85).

For your particular situation, each type of annuity product has positives and negatives. In Chapter 6 we discuss these in detail. As a potential annuity buyer, it is important that you have a basic understanding of the different types of annuities so that you can make the right decision, working with your financial professional, about which type of annuity best fits your particular needs.

CHAPTER 5

WHY BUY AN ANNUITY?

There is much written and reported about annuity products. There are a lot of conflicting messages around them ranging from "don't buy these products under any circumstances" to "you should buy as many of them as possible to eliminate your risk of running out of income as you age." In my opinion, the truth lies in the middle. I believe that annuity products are a very valuable tool that can be used to produce predictable, protected income to maintain a quality lifestyle when you stop full-time work. When used properly, the products reduce financial risks, generate reasonable earnings, create alternative sources of income, and provide the intangible "peace of mind."

To better understand these divergent points of view, let's look into the key reasons why you should or should not buy an annuity. In the end, you will have the information to make the decision for yourself.

THE KEY RISKS ANNUITIES PROTECT AGAINST

In my book *The FinancialVerse – A Common Sense Approach for Your Money*, I identified the eight key financial risks you will encounter in life. My guidance is that you should work to understand and minimize the negative impacts of these risks on your financial life. Annuities can, if used properly, address and work to minimize two of these risks. They are:

1. Longevity Risk – The risk that you live a very long life and won't have the cash income to pay your living expenses. It is the risk

of running out of money in old age when you are unable to work. This risk is a very real concern in our society today.

2.   Health Risk – The risk of becoming ill and not having sufficient resources to pay for the costs of care. This risk includes providing for the cost of long-term care during the later stages of your life should you need it. The long-term care need is the "elephant in the room" for most aging individuals as far as I am concerned. You need cash income in your later years to pay for your share of these costs.

As you design your journey through the stages of the FinancialVerse, you have to plan on addressing these risks using your own financial resources and by the decisions you make. How you approach and solve each risk is a function of your individual circumstances. For example, if by chance you hit the genetic jackpot and your family members normally live to an advanced age, you will need to plan to mitigate longevity risk so that you have the cash to pay the expenses of living a long life. On the other hand, if you are unlucky and inherit poor physical health genes, you will need to plan to have your health risk, and related medical expenses, properly covered. Annuities can also help address this risk.

As I have repeatedly stated in my books and posts, you should not depend on crowd-funding sources such as GoFundMe to mitigate these risks. Crowd funding your financial needs in life, and expecting others to pay for your problems, is a hope and not a reliable or viable strategy. I am not questioning the charitable instincts of people, but how dependable those instincts may be when you need the cash to pay necessary living expenses.

WHY BUY AN ANNUITY?

There are eight key reasons why consumers buy annuities:

1. As a Fixed Income Investment with a Predictable Return – Financial professionals use annuity products as a fixed income asset in clients' financial plans. Almost all annuity products, with the exception of variable and buffered annuities, are designed to offer guaranteed minimum returns or returns tied to the performance of a specified index. The predictability of returns is a key benefit annuities provide and is extremely valuable as you age. For example, if you are 55 years old and suffer major market-related losses, you may not have the time for your portfolio to recover before you stop working. In most interest rate cycles; fixed annuity rates usually pay more than bank CDs. Fixed income assets that are comparable to fixed annuity products would include products such as certificates of deposit, bonds, and money market accounts.

2. As a Source of Tax Deferred Savings – Congress has granted annuity products the benefit of tax-deferred accumulation. Annuities are one of the very few products to be granted this tax advantage along with cash value life insurance, Individual Retirement Accounts (IRAs), 401(k)s, pension plans, and other retirement savings accounts. Tax deferral is a significant advantage in that all income earned by the annuity is deferred until such time that the cash is withdrawn from the contract. This advantage has not been given to stocks, bonds, mutual funds, or any of the other investment products.

    As discussed above, qualified retirement savings plans, like employer-sponsored 401(k) plans, traditional IRAs, and Roth

IRAs, offer the opportunity to save tax deferred. But these plans come with maximum amounts that can be contributed annually and income restrictions for their deductibility. As discussed earlier, there is no limit to the amount of money you can invest into non-qualified annuity products that are purchased with after-tax dollars.

Once an individual has put the maximum amount possible into qualified products such as 401(k)s, IRAs, and other retirement plans, annuity products offer a great place for additional tax-deferred savings. Adding more tax deferral helps consumers maximize compounded accumulation potential—and the more they accumulate, the more income they can generate later in life. If they do not need to access the funds to obtain income, the annuity can be left intact to continue to accumulate until the contract matures. In the low interest environment we are experiencing, this advantage is more valuable than ever.

3. Purchasing a Guaranteed Supplemental Income Stream – As consumers begin their non-working years, they become concerned about the inherent hazards of drawing down too much from their investment portfolio to generate income and depleting savings. This strategy can expose an older individual to market downturns and sequence-of-returns risks (when the market falls early in someone's retirement, making it very difficult—if not impossible—for them to recover). For those beginning, or contemplating retirement, certain annuity products, such as an immediate income annuity, can generate guaranteed income now providing an income floor to complement their withdrawal strategy, generating a supplemental income stream to Social Security, or even filling the income gap until Social Security payments begin.

4. Purchasing a Future Protected Income Stream – Consumers need to know that money invested now will be able to fulfill their cash needs and fund expected longer life expectancies. Certain types of annuity products, such as a fixed index annuity with a lifetime withdrawal rider, can allow them to potentially accumulate more tax-deferred assets and then turn on a stream of income later to cover their cost of living and protect them against the risk of outliving their assets.

5. Purchasing Professional Asset Management – With all annuity contracts, with the exception of variable and buffered annuities, the issuing life insurer is responsible for the management of assets that support the annuity contract. For variable and buffered annuity products, the contract's owner is responsible for investment management. When the life insurer manages the assets, the contract owner benefits from the carrier's actuarial, asset, and risk management capabilities, which individual consumers do not normally possess.

6. Purchasing a Product with Protection of Principal – All annuity contracts, with the exception of variable and buffered annuity contracts, in which you can lose your principal, provide protection for your principal. These contracts have contractual provisions that protect the principal and guarantee minimum annual interest rates. This provision applies to all types of fixed annuity contracts – multiple year, declared rate, and fixed indexed annuities. This guarantee of principal and minimum interest rates differs markedly from equity market products such as stocks and bonds.

7. As an Alternative to Life Insurance if You Can't Qualify – You can use any type of deferred annuity product to provide some of the same benefits as a life insurance policy. But, because an annuity is an investment contract, you don't need to undergo underwriting to qualify for an annuity the way you do for life insurance. If you have a health-related condition that makes life insurance impossible to get or prohibitively expensive, an annuity might be a really good alternative. The annuity will provide:

➤ Ability to automatically pass the full annuity value to your spouse as a beneficiary after your death.

➤ Some annuities offer what are called optional enhanced death benefits that payout a multiple of the annuity's accumulated value upon death of the contract owner. This option is usually available for an additional charge. With these benefits, you won't get as much death benefit as a life insurance product, but you will get some.

8. Source of Partial Long-Term Care Protection – In recent years, life insurance companies have seen a surge in consumer demand for new forms of long-term care protection other than fully underwritten long-term care insurance, which has become much more expensive, limited in available benefits, and harder to qualify for. With people living longer than ever, there is growing concern for long-term care. Here are two options that annuity contracts offer that include a long-term care benefit:

1. **Hybrid Annuity with LTC Benefit** – There are products that offer either an insurance benefit to your heirs or a guaranteed return (albeit small) as the primary function. In the event you needed

nursing home care, then the policy offers a LTC benefit paying a portion of the costs for a determined period of time. The amount and time depend on how much you pay up front and your age. Clients like this option because it's not a sunk cost of paying the full cost of LTC premiums each month and offers some flexibility of getting your money back if you need it.

2. **LTC Benefit that Can Be a Multiple of Your Annuity Account Value** – This benefit, which usually requires some underwriting and is subject to an additional charge, will create a benefit amount to pay for long-term care costs. Some annuities offer a guaranteed enhanced income stream in the form of an income benefit, some carriers will also offer a "LTC multiplier" benefit. How does this work? Let's say that your income benefit is determined to be $20,000 per year from the annuity and you needed LTC care. Instead of $20,000 per year, your benefit would then double to $40,000 per year while you're in the nursing home. This benefit would last for 5 years and then revert back to the original $20,000 annual benefit lifetime income. Every carrier is different so it's important to understand all the moving parts.

These options provide some long-term care coverage and they are not designed to completely pay for 100% of your LTC costs. As consumers are seeing with their own families, having some protection is better than none when it comes to long-term care needs.

WHY AN ANNUITY MIGHT NOT BE RIGHT FOR YOU

As I have stated, annuity products are a tool that have been designed to be a source of tax-deferred accumulation that can generate supplemental income for later in life. They are a valuable tool that can be used in income planning. Hopefully, I have convinced you that annuities *do* have a valuable purpose and can be a great option for some people.

As with any financial product, there are reasons to buy the product and reasons not to. In this book I wanted to objectively show both sides of the coin so that you can decide if the reasons to purchase outweigh the reasons not to buy. Here are seven major reasons not to purchase an annuity product:

1. You **Don't Have Sufficient Savings** – To purchase most annuity products the minimum investment is usually between $10,000 and $100,000 depending on the type of contract. You should only purchase an annuity if the product meets your needs, your liquidity situation and provides diversification of your overall assets.

2. You Want Control Over Your Own Investment Decisions – You may want to make you own decisions over which funds or investment types are part of your annuity. Remember, as a rule, with the exception of variable and buffered annuities, when you buy an annuity product, you will have little to no say over how your money is invested. For variable and buffered annuity products you may be limited to the investment line-up of the insurance carrier, which may not be as broad as you would like. For almost all annuity products the insurance company will usually choose the funds, even the allocations of funds, leaving you little choice as to how the money is invested. If this somehow seems unfair, you have to remember that annuities are primarily designed for people who don't know how or don't want to invest their money. For that type of customer, having control over their investments is a non-concern. If you can, and are

willing to invest your money, even if only through mutual funds and exchange traded funds, you may not need an annuity to get professional asset management. Annuities are excellent for people who either know little about investing or want guaranteed returns.

3. **You Are Not Concerned with Outliving Your Assets** – You could be in a situation where you have accumulated more than sufficient assets to fund the later years of your life. You could also be someone who has control over your spending habits and actual expenditures. As we have said, an annuity is a perfect way to address longevity risk and spending through all of your savings. Annuities are long-term contracts, generally set up specifically to pay out money for the rest of your life. But if, on the other hand, you have a significant amount of accumulated assets and income options an annuity might be restrictive and unnecessary.

4. **You Don't Want to Pay Fees** – All types of annuities can provide many valuable benefits, but they do come with a price. With most variable annuity products, unlike mutual funds (where you can buy the no-load and low-load funds) or certificates of deposit (where there will be no investment fees at all), annuities tend to have several fees associated with them. For variable and buffered annuity products these fees cover investment management, account maintenance, mortality, and expense charges and fees for optional riders. These fees may or may not produce the benefits you are looking for and need to be carefully understood prior to purchasing the contract. All of these fees can reduce your investment and returns if you end up in an annuity that doesn't match your financial situation.

5. **Your Risk Tolerance is Very High** – Annuities are designed to provide bond-like returns (with the exception of variable and buffered annuities where you can get complete or nearly complete equity and bond market exposure). If you are younger than age 50 or have a high-risk tolerance on your investments, annuity products will likely not provide the returns you desire. Additionally, for fixed indexed annuity products these guaranteed returns can come with limited upside gain. For example, though a given market index may return 8% for the index period, the insurance company may cap your return at much lower rates. This may come as a surprise for many people. When they hear index, they think they will receive the full change in the index. There are valid reasons for this, the most important of which is that the insurer has purchased an option supporting the contract that is designed to payout the same way.

6. **Annuity Contracts are Complex** – Annuities do not provide all of the disclosures that come with investment products like mutual funds and exchange-traded funds. When you invest in these funds, you invest your money, the terms and fees are commonly understood, and you can generally exit at any time you like. Annuities are *contracts* that come with numerous contractual stipulations, the costs of which are not separately disclosed. For the most part, those stipulations are put in place based on state regulatory disclosure requirements and to protect the solvency of the insurance company providing the guarantees in the contract. Surrender charges are an excellent example. If you know that you will have to pay a 5% charge in order to liquidate your annuity, you'll probably be unlikely to do so. Such stipulations attach liquidity and tax restrictions to

your investments and remove your ability to make investment changes after the fact without triggering charges or fees. Remember, annuity products are not checking accounts. They are medium to long-term horizon products. They allow limited access to cash for a number of years. Another complication is the sheer number of different annuity products. Each of those annuities has its own provisions and stipulations. Make no mistake about it, annuities can be extremely complicated. Any time you invest money anywhere, you need to be absolutely sure of what it is you're getting into, what specific benefits you will receive, and what risks you are taking on in exchange for those benefits.

7. No Additional Tax-Deferral for Qualified Funds – Much like IRAs and other tax-advantaged retirement saving vehicles, annuities provide tax deferral of your investment earnings, allowing your money to grow without being reduced by annual income taxes. One major difference, however, is that when you purchase an annuity with after-tax dollars, you will not get a tax deduction for your contribution to an annuity the way you will with conventional retirement investments, or if you transfer retirement investments from 401(k)s and IRAs into an annuity product. If you are comfortable with the amount of money that you have in tax-deferred investments, you may have no need to gain additional tax deferral through an annuity. For what it's worth, many financial planners say that at least some of your retirement money should be held outside of tax-deferred accounts. That will give you access to at least some of your money without having to pay taxes on withdrawal.

SUMMARY

Annuities are not for everyone, but there a lot of people who can benefit by owning the right type of annuity product. The key is to understand the risks you are protecting yourself against and how the annuity product works to minimize those risks

CHAPTER 6

THE MAJOR POSITIVES AND NEGATIVES TO BUYING ANNUITIES

In Chapter 2 we discussed the core benefits of all annuity products. Each type of annuity product, however, has specific positives and negatives. Consumers need to understand the benefits and restrictions on what they are buying when purchasing an annuity contract. Overall, in making a purchase, be sure that the benefits to your personal financial situation outweigh the known negatives.

What follows are the major considerations that should be understood for each of the six major annuity product types.

THE POSITIVES AND NEGATIVES OF FIXED ANNUITIES

The Positives

➢ Produce higher returns than many other fixed income options – Fixed annuities usually offer rates of return higher than comparable duration-fixed income products such as certificates of deposit and money market accounts. For example, at the time of writing this book, fixed annuities were offering rates of interest that are at least three times greater than comparable bank accounts and U.S. Treasury securities.

➤ The insurance company manages the investments supporting the annuity – When you buy a fixed annuity, you are buying the money management capabilities of the life insurer issuing the contract. Life insurers manage large portfolios of assets using professional money managers.

➤ Option for guaranteed lifetime income – Fixed annuities possess the contractual option for the purchaser to receive guaranteed income they can't outlive if a lifetime payout option is chosen.

➤ Offer a variety of payout options – Fixed annuities usually offer a number of payout options including receiving payments for a pre-selected number of years.

➤ Tax deferred income accumulation – Fixed annuities offer tax-deferred income accumulation. No current income taxes are due on interest earned by the contract until withdrawn from it. The contract owner gains the advantage of earning additional interest on the amount of taxes not currently paid.

➤ Guaranteed/predictable rates of return – Fixed annuities offer guaranteed rates of interest that are declared at least one year in advance by the life insurance company. The buyer knows exactly the rate of interest they will receive and for what time period. These products appeal to individuals looking for a predictable return.

➤ Principal protection and no risk of principal to market volatility – Fixed annuities are not at risk for market changes due to fluctuations in interest rates or stock market volatility. They protect principal and are not subject to market-related losses.

➤ **All 100% of premiums work to generate interest** – The full amount deposited into a fixed annuity contract begins to earn interest immediately. There are no front-end loads or deductions from the premium deposited.

➤ **Available contract riders** – New fixed annuity products offer contractual riders that can provide optional income or offer benefits that can be used to pay long-term care and nursing home costs.

The Negatives

➤ **Restricted access to cash** – Fixed annuity products are not very liquid. Most fixed annuities allow you to withdraw money from the contract but with restrictions. The three ways to obtain access to cash from fixed annuity products are, 1) by a partial withdrawal from the contract, 2) a full surrender of the contract, and 3) by taking payments based on one of the contract's options and optional riders. If you take more than a certain percentage of the contract's value (usually 10%), you will be subject to a surrender charge. Most annuities come with a surrender charge schedule that requires the buyer to pay a fee if they surrender the annuity contract within a certain number of years (i.e., typically 5 to 7 years). These fees can be significant. So, it's hard to back out of a contract once you purchase it. Overall, only put money into an annuity contract that is being invested or saved for the medium to long term.

➤ **No capital gains tax rates on earnings** – Income earned on fixed annuity contracts is taxed as ordinary income and not as capital gain for income tax purposes. For example, suppose you purchase a fixed annuity contract for $25,000 and surrender the contract 10 years later when its value is $50,000. The gain in the contract of $25,000 will be treated as ordinary income to you and taxed as ordinary income rates in effect at the time of withdrawal.

➤ **Contractual bonuses come with strings attached** – Many annuity contracts are sold with what are advertised as first-year bonus interest of 3% to 5% for example. The buyer should know that to fully earn these bonuses, they will need to hold the contract for a number of years or, in some cases, they will only get the bonus if they take an income stream from the contract.

➤ **Additional income taxes for withdrawals prior to age 59-and-a-half** – If you take withdrawals from a fixed annuity contract prior to age 59½, in most cases, you will need to pay an additional 10% penalty for taking the money out prior to that time in addition to income taxes owned on the withdrawn amount. Remember, annuities were intended to create supplemental retirement income and withdrawals prior to that age trigger this penalty. There are some exceptions to this rule, and you will need to consult your tax professional to get the specifics.

➤ **No additional tax benefit for qualified funds** – If you fund your fixed annuity with pre-tax or qualified funds, you do not receive any additional tax-deferral benefit. Qualified funds are already tax deferred by law and, thus, get no additional income tax benefit by placing these funds into a fixed annuity.

➤ **Complexity** – One of the cardinal rules of saving and investing is not to buy a product you don't understand. Annuities are no exception. Be sure you understand the contract you are purchasing and its key features, benefits, costs and restrictions. Have the financial professional selling you the contract fully explain the contract's key features.

Fixed annuity contracts provide guaranteed fixed rates of return, protection of principal, and guaranteed lifetime income in exchange for certain restrictions. They are a financial tool that you can use to create tax-advantaged returns and supplemental income in your later years.

THE POSITIVES AND NEGATIVES OF VARIABLE ANNUITIES

The Positives

➤ Have the potential to earn higher returns than many fixed income options – Variable annuities have investment options that have the potential to yield more than fixed rates of return as they are typically invested directly in the equity markets.

➤ Option for guaranteed lifetime income – Variable annuities possess the contractually guaranteed option for the purchaser to receive guaranteed income they can't outlive if they chose a lifetime payout option.

➤ Offer a variety of payout options – Variable annuities usually offer a number of payout options including making payments for a pre-selected number of years.

➤ Tax deferred income accumulation – Variable annuities offer tax-deferred income accumulation. No current income taxes are due on interest earned, or capital appreciation by the contract, until withdrawn from it. The owner gains the advantage of earning additional interest on the income taxes not currently paid.

➤ All 100% of premiums go to work to generate interest - The full amount deposited into a variable annuity contract begins to earn interest immediately.

➤ Available contract riders – New variable annuity products offer contractual riders that can provide optional income or offer benefits that can be used to pay long-term care and nursing home costs.

The Negatives

➤ You manage the contract's investments – Remember, with variable annuities, the contract owner is responsible for managing the investments in the contract and the returns generated. You must continually monitor and manage the performance of the investments as this is not the insurance company's responsibility. Variable annuities also restrict investment options to those offered by the life insurance company.

➤ Potentially high ongoing fees – Variable annuities come with a number of annual fees and expenses that can reduce the contract's returns. These fees include administrative costs, mortality and expense fees, investment management fees, and ongoing charges for income rider benefits. The biggest concern with variable annuities is their cost compared to mutual funds and fixed income alternatives.

➤ Restricted access to cash – Variable annuity products are not checking accounts. They are not very liquid. Most variable annuities allow you to withdraw money from the contract but with restrictions. The three ways to obtain access to cash are, 1) by a partial withdrawal from the contract, 2) a full surrender of the contract, and 3) by taking payments based on one of the contract's options. If you take more than a certain percentage of the contract's value (usually 10%), you will be subject to a surrender charge. Most annuities come with a surrender charge schedule that requires the buyer to pay a fee if they surrender the annuity contract in a certain number of years (i.e., typically 5 to 7 years). These fees can be significant. So, it's hard to back out of a contract once you purchase it. Overall, only put money into an annuity contract that is being invested or saved for the medium or long-term.

➤ No capital gains tax rates – Income earned on variable annuity contracts is taxed as ordinary income and not as capital gain. For example, suppose you purchase a variable annuity contract for $25,000 and surrender the contract 10 years later when its value is $50,000. The gain in the contract of $25,000 will be treated as ordinary income for you and taxed at ordinary income rates in effect at the time of withdrawal.

➤ Contractual bonuses come with strings attached – Many annuity contracts are sold with what are advertised as first-year bonus interest of 3% to 5% for example. The buyer would know that to fully earn these bonuses, they will need to hold the contract for a number of years or, in some cases, they will only get the bonus if they take an income stream from the contract.

➤ Additional income taxes for withdrawals prior to age 59½ – If you take withdrawals from a variable annuity contract prior to age 59½, in most cases, you will need to pay an additional 10% penalty for doing so. Remember, annuities were intended to create supplemental retirement income and withdrawals prior to that age trigger this penalty. There are some exceptions to this rule and you will need to consult your tax professional to get the specifics.

➤ No additional tax benefit for qualified funds – If you fund your variable annuity with pre-tax or qualified funds, you do not receive any additional deferral benefit for doing so. Qualified funds are already tax deferred by law and, thus, get no additional income tax benefit by being placed into a variable annuity.

➤ Complexity – One of the cardinal rules of saving and investing is not to buy a product you don't understand. Annuities are no exception. Be sure you understand the contract you are purchasing and its key features, benefits, costs and restrictions.

Variable annuity contracts provide the ability to obtain equity market rates of return, tax-deferred accumulation, access to equity investments, and optional guaranteed lifetime income in exchange for certain fees and restrictions. They are a financial tool that you can use to create tax-advantaged return and supplemental income in your later years.

THE POSITIVES AND NEGATIVES OF BUFFERED ANNUITIES

The Positives

➤ Offer an attractive potential interest return – The potential return is higher than fixed and fixed indexed products but is dependent on the performance of the underlying index options chosen along with the annuity's term and contractual limits. These annuities offer an alternative to variable, fixed, and fixed indexed annuities. People who buy fixed annuities of all types want full downside protection and want to know that they are going to receive a positive return. Fixed indexed annuity holders know their interest crediting strategies change annually but want to protect their principal. Buffered annuity buyers desire more upside participation in exchange for more downside exposure. These products may provide much of the upside that could be captured with a variable annuity (without a living benefit), while still protecting the client from a significant market correction.

➤ The product has been designed primarily for accumulation-focursed buyers.

➤ Premiums deposited in the index options are not directly invested in the equity markets but instead in structured investments, including option contracts, chosen by the life insurance company. The insurance company manages these index investments supporting the annuity. When you buy a buffered annuity, you are buying the money management capabilities of the life insurer issuing the contract. Life insurers manage large portfolios of assets using professional money managers.

➤ Interest crediting strategies do not change within the term selected - These products are usually offered with 1, 3, and 6-year terms that have specific interest crediting calculations. In comparison most fixed indexed annuity contracts allow the issuing life insurer to change how interest is calculated each year. This means that how you participate in the change in the index can be restricted each year. This is a risk you are taking that is implicit in all fixed indexed annuity contracts. This risk does not exist for buffered contracts.

➤ Option for guaranteed lifetime income – Buffered annuities possess the contractually guaranteed options for the purchaser to receive guaranteed income they can't outlive if a lifetime payout option is chosen.

➤ Offers a variety of payout options – Buffered annuities usually offer a number of payout options including receiving payments for a preselected number of years and systematic withdrawals.

➤ Tax-deferred income accumulation – Buffered annuities offer tax-deferred income accumulation. No current income taxes are due on interest earned by the contract until withdrawn from it. The contract owner gains the advantage of earning additional interest on the amount of taxes not currently paid.

➤ All 100% of premiums work to generate interest – The full amount deposited into a fixed annuity contract begins to earn interest immediately. There are no front-end loads or deductions from the premium deposited.

The Negatives

➤ Buffered annuities offer the purchaser limited losses of principal in exchange for restrictions on upside potential – For example, if the contract has what is called a 7% cap and the underlying index increases 10% in one year, the contract holder will be credited with 7% interest for that period. However, if in the next year the contract index decreases 30%, the contract holder would be credited with a loss of 30% limited by the buffer or floor they selected when the product was purchased. You, as the consumer, need to understand you are buying a product that limits your downside risk in exchange for restricted upside potential. Depending upon your age and risk tolerance, this could be a great benefit.

➤ Index returns usually do not include dividends – The index returns for almost all products is based on the pure change in the index and does not include any dividends. This can reduce your returns.

➤ If you chose a floor design, you are exposing yourself to potentially large losses if there is a significant market correction.

➤ Restricted access to cash – Buffered annuity products are not checking accounts. They are not very liquid. Most buffered annuities allow you to withdraw money from the contract but with restrictions. The three ways to obtain access to cash from buffered annuity products are, 1) by a partial withdrawal from the contract, 2) a full surrender of the contract, and 3) by taking payments based on one of the contract's options and optional riders. If you take more than a certain percentage of the contract's value (usually 10%), you will be subject to a surrender charge. Most buffered annuities come with a surrender charge schedule that requires the buyer to pay a fee if they surrender the annuity contract within a certain number of years (i.e., typically 6 years). These fees can be significant. So, it is hard to back out of a contract once you purchase it. Overall, only put money into a buffered annuity contract that is being invested or saved for the medium to long-term.

➤ No capital gains tax rates on earnings – Income earned on buffered annuity contracts is taxed as ordinary income and not as capital gain for income tax purposes. For example, suppose you purchase a contract for $25,000 and surrender the contract 6 years later when its value is $50,000. The gain in the contract of $25,000 will be treated as ordinary income to you and taxed at ordinary income rates in effect at the time of withdrawal.

➤ Additional income taxes for withdrawals prior to age 59½ – If you take withdrawals from a buffered annuity contract prior to age 59½, in most cases, you will need to pay an additional 10% penalty for taking the money out prior to that time, in addition to income taxes owned on the withdrawn amount. Remember, annuities were intended to create supplemental retirement income and withdrawals prior to that age trigger this penalty. There are some exceptions to this rule, and you will need to consult your tax professional to get the specifics.

➤ No additional tax benefit for qualified funds – If you fund your buffered annuity with pre-tax or qualified funds, you do not receive any additional tax deferral benefit for doing so. Qualified funds are already tax-deferred by law and thus get no additional income tax benefit by placing these funds into a fixed annuity.

➤ These products may come with a number of fees that could reduce returns. Buyers should understand all policy-related fees and charges before making a purchase.

➤ Complexity – One of the cardinal rules of saving and investing is not to buy a product you don't understand. Buffered annuities are no exception. They are not as easily understood as mutual funds. Be sure you understand the contract you are purchasing and its key risks, features, benefits, costs, and restrictions.

Buffered annuities could be particularly attractive to clients who currently own variable annuities and/or mutual funds and would like to take some risk off of the table without fully exiting equity markets. They are a financial tool that you can use to create tax-advantaged return and supplemental income in your later years.

THE POSITIVES AND NEGATIVES OF FIXED INDEXED ANNUITIES

As we discussed in Chapter 4, fixed indexed annuities are a type of fixed annuity contract that pays a rate of interest tied to changes in a contractually defined index–such as the S&P 500 index.

The Positives

➤ Offer restricted interest rate upside in exchange for downside protection – The key feature of these products is that they eliminate downside return risk for a cost. They appeal to buyers who are at that stage of their lives when they need more than a pure fixed return but want to avoid portfolio losses.

➤ Offer higher potential returns than many fixed income options – Fixed indexed annuities offer interest-crediting strategies that can yield rates of return higher than comparable duration certificates of deposit, money market accounts and some bonds.

They do not return full equity market rates of return despite their name.

➤ Contractual gains are locked in – Once the contract earns a gain for a year or contractually defined term, that gain is locked in or becomes vested in the contract and cannot be lost.

➤ The insurance company manages the investments supporting the annuity – When you buy a fixed indexed annuity, you are buying the money management capabilities of the life insurer issuing the contract. Life insurers manage large portfolios of assets using professional money managers.

➤ Option for guaranteed lifetime income – Fixed indexed annuities possess the contractually guaranteed option for the purchaser to receive guaranteed income they can't outlive if they chose a lifetime payout option.

➤ Offer a variety of payout options – Fixed indexed annuities usually offer a number of payout options including making payments for a pre-selected number of years.

➤ Tax-deferred income accumulation – Fixed indexed annuities offer tax-deferred income accumulation. No current income taxes are due on interest earned by the contract until withdrawn from it. The owner gains the advantage of earning additional interest on the income taxes not currently paid.

➤ Guaranteed rates of return – Fixed indexed annuities offer interest-crediting strategies at guaranteed rates of interest that are declared at least one year in advance by the life insurance company. The buyer knows exactly the rate of interest they will receive and for what time period. These products appeal to individuals looking for a predictable return.

➤ Principal protection and no risk of principal to market volatility – Fixed indexed annuities offer protection to the principal in the contract from stock market fluctuations.

➤ 100% of premiums to work to generate interest – The full amount deposited into a fixed annuity contract begins to earn interest immediately.

➤ Available contract riders – New fixed indexed annuity products offer contractual riders that can provide optional income or offer benefits that can be used to pay long-term care and nursing home costs.

The Negatives

➤ Limited earnings upside in exchange for no losses on the downside – Fixed indexed annuities offer the purchaser no losses in principal in exchange for limited upside potential. For example, if the contract has what is called a 3% cap and the underlying index increases 10% in one year, the contract holder will be credited with 3% interest for that period. However, if in the next year the contract index decreases 30%, the contract holder would be credited with 0% interest as the contract prohibits any losses. You, as the consumer, need to understand you are buying a product that limits your downside risk in exchange for limited upside potential. Depending upon your age and risk tolerance, this can be very beneficial.

➤ Interest crediting restrictions can change each year – Most fixed indexed annuity contracts allow the issuing life insurer to change how interest is calculated each year. This means that how you participate in the change in the index can be restricted each year. This is a risk you are taking that is implicit in all fixed indexed annuity contracts. Understanding the renewal rate history of the issuing life insurance company will provide you with a historical indicator of how the carrier has treated consumers when setting renewal rates.

➤ Contractual bonuses come with strings attached – Many annuity contracts are sold with what are advertised as first-year bonus interest of 3% to 5% for example. The buyer would know that to fully earn these bonuses, they will need to hold the contract for a number of years or, in some cases, they will only get the bonus if they take an income stream from the contract.

➤ Restricted access to cash – Fixed indexed annuity products are not very liquid. Most fixed indexed annuities allow you to withdraw money from the contract but with restrictions. The three ways to obtain access to cash from fixed annuity products are, 1) by a partial withdrawal from the contract, 2) a full surrender of the contract, and 3) by taking payments based on one of the contract's options and optional riders. If you take more than a certain percentage of the contract's value (usually 10%), you will be subject to a surrender charge. Most annuities come with a surrender charge schedule that requires the buyer to pay a fee if they surrender the annuity contract within a certain number of years (i.e., typically 5 to 7 years). These fees can be significant. So, it's hard to back out of a contract once you purchase it. Overall, only put money into an annuity contract that is being invested or saved for the medium to long term.

➤ No capital gains tax rates – Income earned on fixed indexed annuity contracts is treated as ordinary income and not as capital gain. For example, suppose you purchase a fixed annuity contract for $25,000 and surrender the contract 10 years later when its value is $50,000. The gain in the contract of $25,000 will be treated as ordinary income and taxed at ordinary income rates in effect at the time of withdrawal.

➤ Additional taxes for withdrawals prior to age 59½ – If you take withdrawals from a fixed indexed annuity contract prior to age 59½, in most cases, you will need to pay an additional 10% penalty for taking the money out prior to that time. Remember, annuities were intended to create supplemental retirement income and withdrawals prior to that age trigger this penalty. There are some exceptions to this rule and you will need to consult your tax professional to get the specifics.

➤ No additional tax benefit for qualified funds – If you fund your fixed indexed annuity with pre-tax or qualified funds, you do not receive any additional deferral benefit for doing so. Qualified funds are already tax deferred by law and, thus, get no additional income tax benefit by being placed into a fixed indexed annuity.

➤ Complexity – One of the cardinal rules of saving and investing is not to buy a product you don't understand. Annuities are no exception. Be sure you understand the contract you are purchasing and its key features, benefits, costs, and restrictions.

Fixed indexed annuity contracts provide guaranteed fixed rates of return, potential returns tied to investment market indices, protection of principal and guaranteed lifetime income in exchange for certain restrictions. They offer the potential to earn a higher return than a pure fixed annuity. They are a financial tool that you can use to create tax-advantage return and supplemental income in your later years.

THE POSITIVES AND NEGATIVES OF IMMEDIATE AND DEFERRED INCOME ANNUITIES

The Positives

- Income for life or for the period chosen – Perhaps the most compelling case for an income annuity is that it provides guaranteed income you can't outlive if you chose a lifetime payout option. You cannot purchase guaranteed lifetime income from another source. The only other source of such lifetime income is the Social Security retirement benefit.

- Payments are guaranteed and won't decrease – With income annuities the payment you receive stays the same and will not decrease for your lifetime or a shorter period if you select such. This allows you to plan to use such payments for your life needs. For older individuals looking for a predictable income stream, that may be a better alternative than putting money into equities or even corporate bonds. There are some income annuities that have the ability to increase the payment–these are called increasing payment percentage products–that you can purchase. If you look at these products, you will find that they offer initial payouts that can be substantially lower than products without this feature.

- Investment risk is passed to the insurance company – For income annuities the insurance company assumes responsibility for investing the premium paid for the income annuity and generating the necessary returns to pay the benefits.

The Negatives

- Lack of Liquidity – Once you purchase the income annuity and begin payments, you will, in most cases, not have access to the amount paid for the product. The only exception to this is if you purchase an income annuity with what is called a refund option. The refund option allows you to terminate the contract and receive, as a refund, the remainder of the premium you made for the contract less any payments already received and applicable fees.

- Payments do not increase – Once you purchase an income annuity and begin payments, these payments will not decrease, but they will not increase either. This means that over time, inflation will eat into the value of the payments you are receiving. In high inflation times the value of your payment will be less after a few years. In low inflation times this consideration may not matter as much.

- Low assumed rate of interest on the money invested – Given today's low level of interest rates, by purchasing an income annuity today, you are looking into receiving low rates of interest, which will make your payments lower than if you purchased the product at a time when interest rates were higher.

Overall, income annuities provide you with guaranteed payments for life or shorter time periods selected by you. They have a place in financial planning and risk management. In particular, they provide an income you cannot outlive which you cannot purchase elsewhere.

THE RIGHT MIX OF POLICIES TO BUY

As with any financial tool or product, it may be that you will need to purchase different annuity product types to address your financial risks. After meeting with you and reviewing your financial situation, your financial professional may advise you to purchase different types of annuity products. For example, he or she may recommend that you put part of your assets into an immediate income annuity to provide supplemental income to fund current living expenses, and a separate amount into a fixed or fixed indexed annuity with a lifetime withdrawal benefit to provide lifetime income in 5 to 10 years. You need to understand the product recommendations being made and how they work to mitigate your key financial risks.

SUMMARY

Each of the six types of annuity products has positives and negatives that should be considered when looking to purchase an annuity product. Ultimately, it is up to you and your financial professional to determine, after careful consideration, what each product type offers and whether it is the best solution for your financial needs.

CHAPTER 7

HOW MUCH INCOME SHOULD I PLAN FOR?

AMERICA'S INCOME CHALLENGE

You read almost every week that most Americans have little saved for their ever-lengthening later years. Each of us has this major financial challenge to overcome as we age. That challenge is to have enough income to pay for our living expenses, including healthcare needs, as we age. As we work during what I call in the FinancialVerse our Striving Stage years, we need to accumulate assets, pensions, 401(k) assets, and employment-based benefits that can be used to generate income to pay our bills in later life. At the same time, technology and medical breakthroughs are lengthening our life expectancies. We are seeing more and more people live to the ripe old age of 100. We are pushing back what is considered old age to later and later years. Today's 65-year-old is yesterday's 50-year-old. Fundamentally, we are healthier today and have less chronic health-related issues than prior generations.

The key issue that arises is how are we going to have cash available to pay our living expenses for these longer lifetimes? That is where annuities come in. They provide optional guaranteed income that protects us from running out of money. Protected lifetime income is the major financial and psychological benefit of annuity products. These are great benefits but, as we have seen, they come with a cost and a set of restrictions. Let's take a brief look at how we accumulate assets and benefits for later life, including our country's Social Security retirement program.

THE THREE-LEGGED STOOL OF
SAVINGS FOR THE FULFILLING-STAGE SAVINGS

In the FinancialVerse, you need to accumulate savings and income benefits in order to generate the income you will need in the Fulfilling Stage or later years of your financial life. Remember, once you stop working, you will likely be in this Fulfilling Stage for 20 to 30 years. For younger adults, I believe 30 years should be your planning horizon.

You will accumulate these savings and benefits from three major sources: government programs, employer programs such as 401(k) plans and defined benefit pension plans, and private savings (including annuities and cash-value life insurance). Many licensed financial professionals refer to these programs as the three-legged stool of retirement savings. Let's briefly look at each leg of the stool and what makes it up.

Government Programs

Government programs include Social Security, Medicare, and Medicaid. These programs were designed to provide retirement, disability, and health-cost benefits at certain ages or if certain events take place. A key understanding you must have is that these programs cannot be relied upon to provide the full amount of benefits you will need. For example, Social Security retirement payouts are designed to replace 40% of pre-retirement earnings for most people. **Not 100%, but 40%.** For higher earning individuals, this replacement percentage continues to drop as income earned increases. The average individual Social Security retirement benefit payment was just $1,463 in April 2020 according to Table 2 of the Social Security Administration's Monthly Statistical Report. Could you live on this amount each month?

Medicare provides basic medical coverage for people aged 65 and older, but currently does not cover vision, dental, hearing, or long-term care benefits (it does cover the first 100 days of an extended hospital stay). Medicaid provides health coverage for low-income individuals, children, and the disabled, but the insured has little, if any, say in where the care takes place. Remember, for the most part, the government dictates the specifics of coverage when it is responsible for paying the bill.

These programs are primarily funded and managed by the U.S. Government and the states. The current problem with these plans is that they appear to be substantially underfunded and will need to be modified in the near future. Social Security and Medicare have begun to run deficits – cash outflows are exceeding current contribution inflows. Medicaid programs run by the states now make up in excess of 28.7% of state expenditures, for fiscal 2016, according to the website MACPAC.gov (visited on July 8, 2020). This large percentage now requires cash-strapped state budgets to carefully manage all payments for Medicaid patients.

Upcoming modifications to these programs will likely include a mix of higher contribution rates, some cutback in benefits, lengthening of retirement ages, and some form of income-means testing. These changes are needed in order to assure that all people get the necessary level of benefits from these plans.

I know that many younger adults believe these programs will not exist when they get to the ages to qualify for benefits. My belief is that these entitlement programs are too much of a political issue to be eliminated, but I do believe they could be significantly modified in the future as noted above. I believe you can count on them while planning for the Fulfilling Stage of the FinancialVerse, but you should factor in the reality that their payouts to you will likely be less than you originally planned. This reduction in what these programs offer will place increased pressure on private savings and employer-provided benefits.

Personal Savings - What, When, How Much?

Personal savings are what income, cash, and investments you can accumulate in bank accounts, investments, 401(k) plans, IRAs, cash value life insurance, annuities, and income-generating assets from your earning activities, inheritances, pension plans, or other sources as you go through life. As you focus on savings, it is my belief that you will need to save as much as you can to supplement the future cash you will receive from government and employer programs. As such, you should purchase protection products with the objective of accumulating cash in these products for use in later life or for financial emergencies.

The key guideline that many financial experts discuss is to save at least 10% to 15% of your annual income. I believe, given today's environment, that you should save more if you can. The reason is that there may be years when you cannot put away 10% to 15% and you need to plan for that contingency. You will need all the resources you can accumulate to pay for daily living costs, create an emergency fund, protect against your inability to earn an income, and prepare for the Fulfilling Stage or later years of your life journey.

You need to consider all the available product options, and expense savings techniques, to maximize your personal savings. Permanent life insurance coverage can accumulate cash on a tax-advantaged basis to pay for life's emergencies and to supplement income later in life.

Employer Plans

In the 1970s and 1980s it was normal for the majority of companies to provide what are called defined benefit or pension plans for their employees. These plans were designed to pay an annual cash income benefit of a percentage of the employee's salary after retirement for as long as the employee lived. Individuals used to receive 50% to 60% of their pre-retirement earnings in pension income.

Today, the number of companies providing these types of defined benefit plans has declined dramatically to the point where, according to a March 2018 article (the latest available source) on the website planadvisor.com, only 16% of the Fortune 500 companies offered a defined benefit plan to new hires in 2017, down from 59% in 1998. Almost all employers have replaced these defined benefit plans with what are called defined contribution or DC plans.

Participating in available employer plans is an essential element of accumulating funds for the Fulfilling Stage of your journey and must become a part of your planning. Taking full advantage of any matching funds that your employer will provide to you to assist in paying for later life is a must do.

If you are self-employed, there are tax-advantaged retirement programs in which you can participate and contribute to save for your later years. These plans vary and you will need to consult a tax preparer, investment professional, life insurance professional, or other licensed financial professional to assist you in establishing the plan that is best for you. As more and more people work as independent contractors or only part-time, these plans will gain favor.

THE INCOME REPLACEMENT RATIO

The key question people have to answer is how much of their income they should plan on replacing for the later years of life. Here is how many financial professionals look at this issue. The replacement ratio is a person's gross income after they stop working divided by his or her gross income before this event. For example, assume someone currently earns $60,000 per year from their job. Further, let's assume he or she stops working and receives

$45,000 of Social Security and other income from their 401(k) plan and earnings from personal savings. This person's replacement ratio is 75% ($45,000/$60,000).

Typically, a person usually needs less gross income after they stop working due to several factors:

➤ Income taxes go down in your later years – This is because extra deductions and tax benefits (e.g., real estate tax reductions) are available and taxable income usually decreases when work ceases.

➤ Social Security taxes (FICA deductions from wages) end completely.

➤ Social Security benefits are partially or fully free of federal and state income taxes. This reduces taxable income and, therefore, the amount of income needed to pay taxes.

➤ Other forms of retirement income, like pensions, are often fully or partially exempt from taxation by certain states.

➤ Saving for retirement is no longer needed.

➤ The above savings items are offset by expenses that increase in our later years, such as health-related costs and related insurance premiums.

For all the reasons listed above, conventional wisdom has it that most people will need between 60% to 100% replacement ratio to maintain their standard of living. There is debate in the financial planning community about what percentage to use. For those with lower incomes the ratio can be as high as 100%, while those at very high-income levels may need only 40% of their prior incomes.

The financial problem that arises is matching the level of replacement income you will generate to your living expenses. Many older individuals are finding that their replacement ratio income does not cover their living expenses such that they must sometimes make dramatic changes to their lifestyles.

As people begin to look at their post-work situations, they begin to focus on finding ways to maximize sources of replacement income: Social Security, pensions, and retirement savings (401k, IRA, 403b, 457, etc.). They then realize that they are coming up short and will not achieve the replacement ratio they need to maintain their standard of living. In essence, many people find they cannot stop working as planned or they will need to adapt to a different lifestyle and/or standard of living. That is when they realize the power of annuities as a tool to create income to help them get to the replacement ratio they need.

SUMMARY

The above spells out your income challenge. You must accumulate assets and benefits that are able to pay your living expenses for the years you won't be working. You must generate enough income to keep your standard of living at an acceptable level to pay for the activities you want to participate in in your later years.

CHAPTER 8

FINANCIAL STRENGTH BEHIND THE PRODUCTS

The features, benefits, and guarantees included in annuity products are the financial responsibility - supported by the financial strength - of the life insurance company issuing the annuity contract. It is important that you understand the financial strength of the company you are doing business with. The best way to do this is to understand the financial strength ratings of that company. Here is a brief overview of what you should know.

LIFE INSURER FINANCIAL STRENGTH RATINGS

There are five independent rating agencies – A.M. Best, Fitch, Kroll Bond Rating Agency (KBRA), Moody's, and Standard & Poor's – that provide financial strength ratings for life insurance companies. Each rating agency has its own rating scale, its own rating standards, its own population of rated companies, and its own distribution of company ratings across its scale. Each agency uses numbers, letter grades (e.g., A through F) or pluses and minuses to indicate minor variations in rating from another rating class.

The agencies sometimes disagree about ratings; therefore, you should consider understanding a company's rating from two or more agencies before judging whether to buy or keep a policy from that company. Please note that ratings can change, or are reassessed, at least annually, as the ratings agencies continuously monitor the companies they rate.

Here are practical considerations for looking at financial strength ratings:

➤ Don't rely only on what the insurance companies say about their ratings from these agencies. Companies are likely to highlight a higher rating from one agency and ignore a lower one from another agency, or to select the most favorable comments from a rating agency's report.

➤ To use the ratings from more than one agency, you need to understand that each agency's rating system is different from the others. For example, an A+ from A.M. Best is the next-to-top rating of its 15 categories, but an A+ from Fitch, Kroll or S&P is their 5th-highest rating (out of 24 categories for Fitch, 22 categories for Kroll, and out of 19 categories for S&P). Moreover, Moody's doesn't have an A+ rating. However, the ratings can be classified into "secure" and "vulnerable" mega-categories.

➤ If you like a company's product, I would not do business with any company rated below A- by A.M. Best based on my experience.

RATINGS AGENCY CONTACT INFORMATION

All of the ratings agencies can be found on the Internet as shown below:

Agency	Website
A.M. Best Company, Inc.	www.ambest.com
Fitch Ratings	www.fitchibea.com

Kroll Bond Rating Agency, Inc. (KBRA)	www.kbra.com
Moody's Individual Service	swww.moodys.com
Standard & Poor's Insurance Ratin	gwww.standardandpoors.com

STATE GOVERNMENT GUARANTY FUNDS

In addition to the financial strength rating of life insurance carriers, there is a non-publicized backstop that kicks in if a company runs into financial trouble and becomes insolvent and is unable to pay its claims and obligations to policyholders. This has been a very rare event for companies offering annuity products, but it does happen periodically. The backstop that I refer to are the state guaranty associations. Let's look at what they are and how they stand behind the policy you buy.

Insurance guaranty associations provide protection to insurance policyholders and beneficiaries of policies issued by an insurance company that has become insolvent and is no longer able to meet its financial obligations. All states, the District of Columbia, and Puerto Rico have insurance guaranty associations. Insurance companies are required by law to be members of the guaranty association in states in which they are licensed to do business. These associations cover policies for annuities, individual and group life insurance, long-term care, and disability income insurance.

In the very rare event that an insurance company has insufficient assets to pay policyholder claims, a guaranty association will obtain funds by assessing member insurers that write the same kind of business as the insolvent insurer. These assessments (together with the assets of the insurer) are then used to pay, up to statutory limits (see below), the covered claims of policy-holders of the insolvent company. An association may also provide continued coverage for the policyholder or transfer policies to healthy insurers.

The guaranty association's coverage of insurance company insolvencies is funded by post-insolvency assessments of the other guaranty association member companies. These assessments are based on each member's share of premium they have written in that state during the prior three years.

The amount of coverage provided by the guaranty association is set by state statute and differs from state to state. The limits are just that–limited cover-age–and, in some cases, will not provide full protection for the policy you purchased. Most states provide the following amounts of coverage (or more):

- $300,000 in life insurance death benefits

- $100,000 in net cash surrender or withdrawal values for life insurance

- $250,000 in present value of annuity benefits, including cash surrender and withdrawal values (payees of structured settle-ment annuities are also entitled to $250,000 of coverage)

- $300,000 in long-term care insurance benefits

- $300,000 in disability income insurance benefits.

During the sales process, you will find that your agent or direct provider will not discuss the state guaranty associations as they are normally prohibited from doing so. As an educated buyer, you should know how the associations work in your state. To accomplish this, you should contact the state insurance department or state guaranty association for the state in which you are res-ident with questions about coverage and exclusions.

SUMMARY

....

When you purchase an annuity contract, the primary entity supporting the financial obligations and guarantees in the contract is the life insurer issuing the contract. Life and annuity insurers are heavily regulated by their state of domicile. In addition, almost all the life and annuity insurers are rated for their financial strength by a group of five major rating agencies. In the rare and unfortunate situation where an insurer has financial problems and must be rehabilitated, there is a system of state-based guaranty funds serving as a backup that will cover a portion of the contract's benefits.

CHAPTER 9

WHERE TO BUY
AND THE BUYING PROCESS

THE CASH SAVINGS NEEDS HIERARCHY

Before we discuss the aspects of the annuity buying process, I think it's important to cover some basics with you about saving and investment. It begins with setting up a savings account and ends with making investments. I believe this is an important series of steps to review before making any insurance contract or investment purchase, particularly in purchasing an annuity product. Please know that I am not a licensed investment professional and offer my comments as common sense practical thoughts about the savings and investment process.

To help in reviewing the savings and investment process, I have developed what I call the Cash Savings Needs Hierarchy for your consideration. I have tried to come up with a simple approach to a very personal decision process. After you are able to comfortably pay your basic needs each month, including debt service, and can see that you have extra cash in your checking account each month, you are ready to implement the Cash Savings Needs Hierarchy. It is a rational process with the following steps:

1. Establishing an online savings account – Online accounts typically pay significantly higher rates of interest on your savings

than offerings from the brick-and-mortar financial institutions and are easy to get money from if needed. Use this account to begin to accumulate your excess cash and segregate it from your checking account so that you are not tempted to spend the money. One way to do this is to set up regular transfers from your checking account to the online savings account.

2. Use the online savings account to build your emergency fund – Remember, as I have discussed in the FinancialVerse books, you need to create a fund of at least $10,000 or six months of basic living expenses. Keeping your emergency fund in an account that you can draw on quickly, if needed, should give you peace of mind.

3. I know that once you have accumulated your emergency account, the questions of whether you should repay debt, purchase a home, go on a big travel adventure or make a dream purchase will arise in your mind. Accelerating debt payments would be my personal choice. Being free of the negative impact of debt payments is as liberating a financial event than any other. Take a look at the work of Dave Ramsey and his books in this area to help you on this journey. As far purchasing a home is concerned, there is, in my view, no easy answer as to whether this is the right thing to do. In certain regions of the country, it is better to own versus rent your home while in other areas purchasing a home is almost impossible. You will need to speak with real estate and financial professionals to determine the best course of action in your area. Taking that dream trip or buying a collection of vintage guitars are personal choices. Once you have established a foundation of having an emergency fund, the choice is yours.

4. Begin to fund your 401(k) plan if one is available to you at work. Remember, the sooner you start saving, the greater impact it will have on your retirement. Many people miss out using the 401(k) plan offered by their employer and the matching contribution offered. Most employers match your contributions up to a certain level. According to a 2019 report from Fidelity investments, the majority of employers match your contributions up to 4.7% of your salary, although, some companies have stopped matching contributions as a result of the financial impacts of COVID-19. Remember, 401(k) employer matching funds are like found money. If you can save 4.7% of your salary and the employer matches that amount, you would be saving 9.4% of your salary for your later years, which is a heathy start on what you should be putting away.

5. After you have your emergency fund set up, and are fully funding your 401(k), I would look to take the excess and fund one of three needs depending upon your individual situation. These would include:

➤ Cash value life insurance with the goal of accumulating funds for later in life and creating permanent life insurance coverage.

➤ Setting up a Health Savings Account, if you qualify based on the type of health insurance you have.

➤ Lastly, I would begin to fund a 529 College Savings Plan for any dependent children you have.

6. If you still have cash left after fully funding steps 1 through 4, I would then meet with a financial professional to develop a plan to begin to invest for the future as agreed with the professional.

A qualified financial professional can work with you to determine what products best meet your risk and return needs.

When you reach step 5 and you have accumulated a reasonable level of savings, it may be time to consider the purchase of an annuity product. For most people, based on today's reality, that time comes in their late 40s or early 50s. One of the reasons for this age range is the basic nature of annuity products. They are mostly fixed-return investments that offer protection of principal. When you are in your 50s, it is harder and harder for you to overcome a large decline in the equity markets. If the market drops 50%, you have fewer years to recover from the loss and still make your retirement goals.

PAYING FOR YOUR ANNUITY

As you prepare to purchase an annuity, there are three usual ways to pay for the product:

> ➤ Using a check drawn from money available in taxable accounts, such as non-qualified bank and brokerage accounts. Remember, there is no limit to the amount you can invest in an annuity contract with after-tax funds.

> ➤ Using money drawn from existing qualified or tax-deferred accounts. There are limits set by the Internal Revenue Service on the annual amounts that can be invested into a qualified annuity contract. For example, if you were going to use the annuity as your IRA contribution for a given year, you would be limited by the income and amount restrictions for the IRA for that year.

> ➤ By rolling over the surrender value from an annuity you already own into another annuity contract using the provisions of Section 1035. This is called a 1035 Exchange in the business. There is no limit to the amount you can rollover into an annuity product, but there are restrictions and requirements as to how and when the rollover must take place.

These are the key sources of cash used to purchase annuity products.

THE PLACES YOU'LL LOOK – THE PURCHASE CHANNELS

Now that you have reviewed your savings and investment situation and have decided to look into purchasing an annuity product, let's dive into where you can purchase these products.

The first thing to remember is that annuities are classified as life insurance products and can only be sold by a financial professional that has been properly licensed. This means they are properly licensed to do business by the state in which you reside, have taken the courses necessary to sell annuity products, and have taken any product-related training for the insurance carriers they represent. If you are looking to purchase a variable or buffered annuity product, the individual must also hold specific credentials from the Securities and Exchange Commission and be a properly licensed securities professional.

You can purchase an annuity product from the following sources and individual designations:

> ➤ Captive or Career Insurance Agents – These are employees or agents of a single life insurance company. Usually, they sell the products of only that insurance company.

➤ Banks and Savings and Loans–Investment Counselors – Banks and savings and loans will sell the products of three to five insurance companies that have been approved by their employer for sale.

➤ Investment Brokers–Account Executives, Registered Representatives – These are securities and life, licensed individuals who sell the annuity products that have been approved by their designated broker dealer.

➤ Financial Planning Firms–Financial Advisers and Investment Counselors – Some financial planning firms allow their advisers to sell products in addition to providing financial planning services.

➤ Independent Insurance Agents – These agents are licensed to sell life insurance and annuities and may not be licensed to sell securities products. Most independent agents offer the annuity products of three to five life insurance companies.

➤ Registered Investment Advisors – These individuals are registered with the Securities and Exchange Commission and are also licensed to sell annuity products many a times.

➤ Direct Online – These sites offer annuity products sold by online agents without a face-to-face sales meeting. Direct sales are in their infancy and are offered by certain life insurance companies. These individuals may offer a smaller set of products for sale. The reason that direct sales are just beginning for annuity products is that most people would prefer to meet with and speak directly to a salesperson when they are making what, on average, is about an $80,000 purchase of an annuity product.

➤ At work through payroll benefits – Some companies offer annuity products through payroll deduction plans or as offerings under 401(k) plans. There are also specific annuity products available under what are called 403(b) plans offered by certain public schools and tax-exempt organizations. These products have specific benefits and restrictions.

QUESTIONS TO ASK BEFORE YOU BUY

By this time, you have an understanding of how annuities work and how they can help you mitigate key financial risks. As you look at various product solutions recommended by your qualified financial professional, you need to make sure you clearly understand the product you are purchasing and the key features of the annuity. Here are my thoughts on the 10 key areas you must understand before making the purchase.

What is the Type of Annuity Being Recommended and Why?

Be sure you understand how the type of annuity being recommended fits your risk appetite and how it will address the financial risks you are seeking to mitigate. As described in Chapter 2, there are numerous key benefits to annuity products. In Chapter 4 we reviewed the six major product types and when they are most often purchased, and in Chapter 6 we discussed the positives and negatives of each product type.

How Interest is Credited to the Annuity Contract?

I know it sounds rather simple, but you need to understand how you will earn interest/return on your annuity investment. Have the financial professional walk you through how interest is calculated and how it is credited to your contract. This is especially important for fixed indexed, buffered, and variable annuity products that have a number of different crediting strategies.

What Are the Surrender or Withdrawal Charges for Deferred Annuities?

Deferred annuity contracts almost always come with a surrender charge period and charge amounts. As we discussed in Chapter 1, these charges can last for 5 to 7 years and can be substantial. Remember, surrender charges are an integral part of deferred annuity contracts. You cannot escape buying a contract with such charges. Be sure you understand the amount and length of such charges.

What Are the Fees and Annual Charges?

For any product you purchase, particularly for buffered and variable annuities, be sure that the financial professional reviews with you all charges for investment management, administration, death benefits, and charges for all optional riders. These fees and charges can really eat into your return and you must make an informed decision that you are incurring them for the right risk-reduction reasons.

How Can You Access Cash in the Contract?

For all annuity types, including immediate and deferred income annuities, you need to understand how you can gain access to cash in the contract in case you have a financial emergency. During the information gathering process, your financial professional will be asking you questions regarding your cash liquidity needs. Please understand your contractual rights to full withdrawals, partial withdrawals, annuitization options, death benefits, and optional lifetime withdrawal benefits. As I have stated repeatedly in this book, annuities are not checking accounts. They are medium to long-term products. If you need full access to the deposit you are making to buy the annuity contract as a source of emergency funds, you should not be buying this product.

Who Is the Issuing Life Insurance Company?

As presented in Chapter 8, the primary party financially responsible for the benefits and guarantees made in the annuity is the issuing life insurance company. You need to know the financial strength ratings of the company. My advice is not to purchase a contract from a company rated less than A- from A.M. Best.

What are The Options to Receive Income?

You need to fully understand all the options you are granted by the contract and any riders you purchase to receive income from the annuity contract. Have your financial professional walk you through each option.

What Are the Optional Riders and Related Costs?

If you elect to purchase optional riders, such as a lifetime withdrawal benefit, long-term care benefits, or an enhanced death benefit, be sure you understand what events trigger your eligibility for the benefit, how you elect to receive the benefit, what documentation you may need to provide (i.e., evidence of a long-term care event), any fees or costs for using the benefit, and the impact on how the annuity accumulates cash value if you begin receiving benefits under an optional rider.

Where to Contact for Service Issues?

An overlooked set of questions has to do with getting the contact information (e.g., telephone numbers, website addresses or email addresses) for the policyholder service department of the issuing insurance company. Be sure to get this information and put it in your files so that it can be readily accessed.

How Much is the Selling Agent Receiving in Commission on your Purchase?

The financial professional selling you the annuity contract should disclose the compensation they are receiving for selling you the product. There are changing regulatory requirements that are now forcing all agents to disclose this information, but the requirements differ by state. If your selling financial professional does not disclose the amount of compensation they will receive, you need to ask. As I have stated, I do not object to commissions being paid, but I do believe they should be disclosed.

THE FIVE STEPS TO PURCHASING AN ANNUITY

There are five steps involved in the purchase of an annuity. The process is simple and easy to follow. Here they are:

1. Meet with your licensed financial professional. During this meeting, the professional will ask you questions and gather information regarding your risk tolerance, financial information, liquidity

needs, annuity features needed, and other information that may be required by the state you live in or by the insurance carrier.

2. The agent will complete the annuity application using information you provided for your signature. The application will need to be signed by you along with certain state and life insurance company disclosure forms. You will be asked to produce a check if you are purchasing the contract using non-qualified funds, transfer forms if you are funding the annuity from qualified sources, or mandated paperwork evidencing a 1035 Exchange of one annuity product you already own for the new purchase.

3. The agent will submit your application to the annuity carrier for approval. The annuity carrier will review the documentation submitted and may reach out to you or the agent on your behalf for additional information or clarification regarding information provided. Since there is no underwriting of the annuity contract, once the documentation is reviewed and accepted by the life insurance company, the annuity purchase is approved.

4. The life insurance company approves the application and issues the full annuity contract directly to you or to your agent for delivery. Upon delivery, you may be required to acknowledge receipt of the contract by signing a delivery form or receipt. From the time an annuity contract is delivered you will have between 10 to 30 days - the time varies by state requirement - to reconsider your purchase decision and send the contract back for a full refund. This 10 to 30 day period is called the "free look" period and has been designed by state regulators to give you time to rethink your purchase. After the free-look period is over, the annuity contract's surrender charge/penalty provisions become fully effective.

5. Once you have finally agreed to the purchase, place the annuity contract in a safe place, such as a bank safe deposit box. Also, please make note of the key web addresses, customer service telephone numbers, and mailing addresses for service matters. These will come in handy if you need to trigger any of the contract's benefits or need to surrender the contract.

Just five easy steps to make the purchase. For most annuity carriers in the market today, this entire process from application submission to contract delivery should take place in less than 10 business days.

HOW MUCH DO ANNUITY SALESPEOPLE EARN ON MY PURCHASE?

The question of what the selling agent will make in commissions or compensation on the sale is one of the most frequently asked and most controversial. A selling agent, from all buying sources, will receive compensation in one form or other from your purchase. The agent usually has the option of receiving the compensation at the time of contract issuance in a lump sum, a smaller amount upfront with an amount paid out over the time you hold the contract, or an amount charged to you each year and paid as a separate fee taken as a direct deduction from the annuity contract.

The amounts of compensation earned varies depending on the type of annuity purchased. Upfront commissions can be as high as 6% to 1% or less for those professionals charging annual fees for their continued advice to you. You can easily see that if you are going to hold the annuity for a long-term – say 10 years – the amount paid in annual fees can greatly exceed an upfront commission of 6%. My advice is to ask the salesperson what they are being paid on the sale if it is not disclosed to you during the sales process. One last point that has to do with annuities purchased from direct sources - just because an annuity is purchased directly via the Internet, does not mean it is priced without commission. The marketing company and the issuing life insurer have to pay the full cost of advertising, marketing costs, technology, and salesforce compensation as part of the direct sale. These costs have to be covered by the product and will be reflected in the product's price.

SUMMARY

Annuity products can be purchased from a growing number of sources ranging from banks to online channels. Finding a financial professional who walks you through the purchase process and works to deliver the best product solution for your needs is your best outcome. The buying process, once you know the product you need, is straightforward and easy to complete. As always, fully answer all questions asked of you by the financial professional and in all disclosure forms.

CHAPTER 10

YOUR NEXT STEPS

Now that you have read this book, you may have decided that an annuity fits into your financial needs and you would like to begin the process of purchasing the product. To help you, I have prepared some resources for you to use.

PERFORMING AN INCOME CHECK-UP

In Resource Checklist 1, I have included the FinancialVerse Fulfilling Stage Income Check-Up form for you to complete. This form has been created to help you think through the key matters before you meet with a financial professional to discuss buying the product. The form provides a very basic way to look at your living expenses, your expected income, and what income replacement ratio you will need. It also presents some key considerations you should look at as time moves closer to the end of your full-time work life. At a minimum, it will prepare you for your meeting with the financial professional you choose.

MAKING THE PURCHASE

You can now begin the buying process using the suggestions contained in Chapter 9.

KEEPING THE POLICY IN-FORCE

Annuity products differ from other life insurance products, as they are mostly purchased with a one-time single premium. There is no need to make subsequent premium payments to keep the policy in force. Once purchased, all you need to do is to keep your contact and beneficiary information up to date. Almost all annuity issuers will allow you to do this electronically through their websites with proper identification. A major piece of advice is to keep your beneficiary information current such that the proceeds from the annuity are directed to the right source if an unplanned event takes place.

FILING A CLAIM FOR BENEFITS

With today's annuity products offering more and more core and optional benefits, you must understand what documentation will be required from you by the issuing carrier to collect benefits. Your financial professional, who sold you the contract, can be an excellent resource in filing a claim or you can deal directly with the policyholder service department of your annuity carrier. Please be sure to comply with all carrier-required requests for documentation, as this will speed the approval process for your payments.

SUMMARY

You have come a long way in your journey to understand annuity products and how they are a tool to help you mitigate financial risks. Your next steps are all up to you. Being prepared for life's later years and expected longer life expectancies is one of the best things you can do in the FinancialVerse to reduce financially created stress and anxiety.

CHAPTER 11

FINAL THOUGHTS / SHOULD YOU BUY AN ANNUITY?

If you have stayed focused and read the information I have presented in this book, you should clearly understand that annuities are a financial tool that can be used to reduce key financial risks that you face in the FinancialVerse. They provide certain guarantees that you cannot buy in other financial products. Here are some of the major thoughts that I hope you have learned and understand about these products:

➤ Annuities have been around for centuries and have been available in the United States since the 18th century.

➤ Almost every American owns at least one annuity, although they may not realize they do. That annuity is their Social Security retirement benefit. Each person owns a flexible premium, partially inflation adjusted income annuity that begins paying at certain ages. Remember, Social Security retirement benefits have been designed to payout a benefit equal to about 40% of the average worker's salary once they meet the age thresholds to start payments.

➤ Annuity products have been granted certain tax advantages, including tax deferral on all earnings, by Congress as incentives to save and invest for the time you are not working full time. Congress and the Internal Revenue Service have also placed certain restrictions on the products including penalties for taking withdrawals early and the taxation of all contract earnings at ordinary income tax rates as part of granting the product with tax-deferred accumulation.

➤ Annuity products can help minimize the risk of outliving an individual's assets as they age. This is done by providing guaranteed, protected streams of lifetime income.

➤ There are several key annuity product types including income and deferred annuities.

➤ Annuity contracts earn income in three ways: fixed, indexed, and variable rates of return.

➤ Annuity products have certain key characteristics that you must understand, including limited access to contractual amounts, tax restrictions, and surrender charges.

➤ Annuities are primarily used to generate supplemental income for the later years of an individual's life. They create an income stream that, when added to other income sources (e.g., Social Security, pensions, and payouts from private savings), enable individuals to maintain desired standards of living in their non-working years.

➤ Annuities have a number of significant positives and negatives that the buyer needs to understand before purchasing an annuity. All of these items should be understood before making a purchase.

➤ There are a great number of educational and support resources available to assist you in making your purchase. From resources provided by insurance carriers, national research organizations to licensed financial professionals in your local area, these entities are there to assist you in your purchase journey.

➤ Purchasing the right amount and mix of annuity products is part of building your financial foundation to provide cash for future delivery for your own unique needs. Like any product, you should not have the majority of your net worth tied to these contracts and should work with a financial professional to make sure you have a diversified portfolio of assets with sufficient liquidity.

➤ Today's annuity products have been improved to include the additional benefits that allow surrender charge free access to the policy's value for triggering events such as being diagnosed with a terminal illness, nursing home confinement, having a long-term care event. These benefits are not fully understood by consumers as being offered by annuity products.

➤ You need to exercise caution when buying the product by knowing the type and duration of annuity you are buying, the related costs of the contract, and the financial strength of the insurance company whose product you are purchasing.

➤ In addition to the insurance carrier you are purchasing the product from, a state guaranty fund has been established to pay a certain dollar amount of claims if your insurance carrier becomes insolvent. Please understand your state's guaranty fund provisions and limitations.

➤ The buying process has five major steps that are understandable and routine. Please remember to be truthful and timely with any questions, documentation, and payments you are asked to make.

> When the time comes to file a claim benefit under the policy you have purchased, please be sure to accurately and fully complete what is asked of you.

I thank you for taking the time and making the investment to learn about today's annuity products and how they can be used to reduce your financial risks in the FinancialVerse. My best wishes to you as you seek to continue to improve your knowledge of money and how to manage it to provide the life you want. Remember – when in doubt, ask for help. There are a great number of licensed and professionally trained licensed financial professionals and organizations who are ready to help.

RESOURCE CHECKLISTS

RESOURCE CHECKLIST 1 - PERFORMING A FULFILLING STAGE INCOME CHECK-UP

As you develop a strategy for your Fulfilling Stage and begin living in it, it is important to routinely estimate your expenses and determine how much income you'll need to live comfortably. It is never too early or too late to start! This simple guide may help you identify your needs and develop the information necessary to create a strategy for your future. It also provides you with a checklist you can use whether you are years, months, or days away from your retirement date.

FULFILLING STAGE INCOME WORKSHEET

Start with this three-part worksheet to find out how financially ready you are for the Fulfilling Stage and to identify areas to help you be better prepared.

PART 1: IDENTIFY YOUR ESSENTIAL
EXPENSES AND LIFESTYLE EXPENSES

Use this chart to pinpoint your current monthly expenses.

Essential Expenses	Amount	Lifestyle Expenses	Amount
Housing	$	Dining Out	$
Utilities	$	Clothing	$
Healthcare	$	Hobbies	$
Transportation	$	Entertainment	$
Groceries	$	Personal Care	$
Insurance (Life and Other)	$	Charitable Giving	$
Debts	$	Gifts	$
Income Taxes	$	Professional Services	$
Other	$	Other	$

Total Current Monthly Expenses: $_____

PART 2: DETERMINE YOUR FULFILLING STAGE INCOME

Use this worksheet to inventory the amount of monthly income you expect
to receive from all sources.

Source	Amount	Source	Amount
Pension	$	Roth IRA	$
Social Security	$	Brokerage Account	$
Fixed Annuities	$	Other Savings	$
Variable Annuities	$	Life Insurance Cash Value	$
Veteran's Benefits	$	Home Equity	$
Long-Term Bonds	$	Employment Income	$
Rental Income	$	Interest Dividends	$
Employee Savings Plans	$	Municipal Bonds	$
Traditional IRA	$	Other	$

Total Monthly Fulfilling Stage Income: $_____

PART 3: CALCULATE YOUR INCOME REPLACEMENT RATIO

You have estimated your current monthly expenses and sources of retirement income. How do you think these current expenses will compare to your needs in retirement? Do you expect the amount of these expenses to be the same, lower, or higher during your retirement years? How much ordinary income will you need to replace with retirement income?

Consider this when you are evaluating your replacement ratio. Most experts agree you will need anywhere between 60% to 85% of your pre-retirement earnings to maintain your desired standard of living. So, your personal replacement ratio will depend on how you want to live during retirement. Consider the following examples based on $100,000 of annual pre-retirement income, which is $8,333 monthly income.

- ❏ If you want to live more modestly than you did before retirement, your replacement ratio will be lower than 100%. Example: 70% replacement ratio = $5,833 monthly income ($70,000 annually).

- ❏ If you want to maintain your current lifestyle, your replacement ratio will be 100%. Example: 100% replacement ratio = $8,333 monthly income ($100,000 annually).

- ❏ If you want to live larger than your current lifestyle, your replacement ratio will be more than 100%. Example: 120% replacement ratio = $10,000 monthly income ($120,000 annually).

    Total Monthly Retirement Expense: _____ / Total Current Monthly Income: _____ =

    Estimated Replacement Ratio: _____%

How long until you retire? Use this checklist to develop a strategy for your retirement as you work towards the big day.

A Few Years Before You Retire . . .

- ❏ Define your Fulfilling Stage goals

- ❏ Maximize contributions to retirement accounts

- ❏ Take advantage of catch-up contributions

- ❏ Ensure at least a portion of your income is protected

- ❏ Plan ahead for potential long-term care expenses

- ❏ Pay down debts

As You Get Closer to the Fulfillment Stage . . .

- ❏ Review your benefits including healthcare benefits (if available)

- ❏ Evaluate and document your workplace retirement plan(s)

- ❏ Gather information about your Social Security benefits

- ❏ Investigate your Medicare coverage and Medicare Supplement options

- ❏ Pinpoint gaps in your healthcare, income, and other important benefits

- ❏ Reassess and estimate your income needs

- ❏ Create a "Plan B" for the unexpected (illness, unplanned work event, income gaps)

- ❏ Continue to save

- ❏ Continue to pay down debts

About A Year Before Your Enter the Fulfilling Stage . . .

❏ Choose your expected start date

❏ Set up your budget based on estimated expenses and income replacement ratio

❏ Consider consolidating some of your retirement accounts

❏ Determine if you would like to work (new career, part-time, consulting, etc.)

❏ Set your Fulfillment Stage goals (and discuss them with your spouse or partner

A Few Months Before You Enter the Fulfilling Stage . . .

❏ Inform your employer you intend to cease work and fill out the necessary paperwork

❏ Talk with Human Resources about your retirement plan options and/or stock options

❏ Ask for an income estimate from your pension company (if applicable)

❏ Create a withdrawal strategy that helps ensure your income will last all the years you live in retirement

❏ Apply for Medicare if it is three months before your 65th birthday

❏ Set an age to begin taking Social Security

❏ Consider meeting with a tax advisor and/or attorney to map out your tax strategy and/or estate plan

Enter the Fulfilling Stage!

❏ Congratulations! Pat yourself on the back!

❏ Have a party!

After You Have Entered the Fulfilling Stage . . .

❏ Continue to follow your income strategy

❏ Re-evaluate your goals and income strategy as your circumstances change

❏ Routinely review your beneficiaries to ensure they are correct and up to date

❏ Work with your tax professional to take care of your tax obligations and watch for IRS forms/reporting issue

After completing the worksheet and checklists, how prepared do you feel? What things can you do now to live comfortably in the Fulfilling Stage later? What questions do you have?

Whether you are years, months, or days away from entering the Fulfilling Stage, a financial professional can help answer many of your questions and offer useful tips.

Please note that a financial professional with an insurance license only may not do financial planning. Please ask your financial professional about whether he/she has the licensing to help with financial planning.

This informational publication is designed to provide general information on the subjects covered. Pursuant to IRS Circular 230, it is not, however, intended to provide specific legal or tax advice and cannot be used to avoid tax penalties or to promote, market, or recommend any tax plan or arrangement. Please note that FinancialVerse, its affiliated companies, and their representatives and employees do not give legal or tax advice. You are encouraged to consult your tax advisor or attorney.

Any transaction that involves a recommendation to liquidate a securities product, including those within an IRA, 401(k), or other retirement plan, for the purchase of an annuity or for other similar purposes, can be conducted only by individuals currently affiliated with a properly registered broker/dealer or registered investment advisor. If your financial professional does not hold the appropriate registration, please consult with your own broker/dealer representative or registered investment advisor for guidance on your securities holdings.

Annuities are designed to meet long-term needs for retirement income. They provide guarantees against the loss of principal and credited interest, and the reassurance of a death benefit for beneficiaries.

Not affiliated with the U.S. government or a governmental agency.

This informational publication is not approved, endorsed, or authorized by the Social Security Administration.

RESOURCE CHECKLIST 2 - RESOURCE ORGANIZATIONS

As you research annuity products and information, here are organizations and their website addresses that I have found useful:

1. *Financial Industry Regulatory Authority (FINRA)* – www.finra.org. FINRA is a government-authorized not-for-profit organization that oversees U.S. broker-dealers. Its website has valuable information and tools you may find of value.

2. *Securities and Exchange Commission (SEC)* – www.sec.gov. The SEC is part of the Federal government with the mission to protect investors; maintain fair, orderly, and efficient markets; and facilitate capital formation. The SEC strives to promote a market environment that is worthy of the public's trust.

3. *United States Department of the Treasury* – www.ustreas.gov. The U.S. Department of the Treasury's mission is to maintain a strong economy and create economic and job opportunities by promoting the conditions that enable economic growth and stability at home and abroad, strengthen national security by combating threats and protecting the integrity of the financial system, and manage the U.S. Government's finances and resources effectively. It is the organization that oversees the Internal Revenue Service.

4. *The Internal Revenue Service* – www.irs.gov. The Internal Revenue Service is the nation's tax collection agency and administers the Internal Revenue Code enacted by Congress. On its website you can locate valuable information about annuity products.

5. *American Council of Life Insurers (ACLI)* – www.acli.org. The ACLI advocates on behalf of 280 life insurance company members dedicated to providing products and services that promote consumers' financial security. ACLI represents member companies in state, federal and international forums for public policy that supports the industry marketplace and the families that rely on life insurers' products for peace of mind. ACLI members represent 95% of life insurance industry assets in the United States.

6. *The Secure Retirement Institute* - https://www.loma.org/Solutions/ SRI.aspx. The Secure Retirement Institute provides comprehensive, unbiased research and education covering all aspects of the

retirement industry. The Secure Retirement Institute's goal is to spur innovation and broaden industry collaboration to help improve retirement readiness and promote retirement security. It is an excellent resource for information on industry annuity sales, key consumer trends and current industry developments.

7. *The National Association for Fixed Annuities (NAFA)* – www.nafa. com. The National Association for Fixed Annuities, or NAFA, is a national trade association exclusively dedicated to promoting the awareness and understanding of fixed annuities. NAFA is the only association whose sole purpose is to advocate for fixed annuities and educate the public, as well as regulators and legislators, about the benefits fixed annuities have for those in or planning for retirement. Members of NAFA include more than 80 insurance carriers and independent marketing organizations that represent 200,000+ agents and registered representatives who sell fixed annuities. Relying on the support of each and every one of them, NAFA helps to protect consumers by guiding its members to adhere to the highest standards of market conduct and ethical behavior.

8. *The Insured Retirement Institute (IRI)* – www.irionline.org/. IRI is the leading financial services trade association for the retirement income industry. Members represent the entire supply chain of insured retirement strategies, including insurers, banks, asset managers, broker-dealers, distributors, financial advisors and solution providers. IRI provides a wealth of educational and research materials on retirement and annuity products.

ABOUT THE AUTHOR

Harry N. Stout is a published author and former financial services executive with over 20 years' experience in all aspects of annuity product development, sales and service. A certified public accountant by training, he has worked in various countries helping consumers save, financially protect their families, and prepare for the later years of their lives. He has been the President and/or Chief Executive Officer of several large U.S. life insurance and annuity businesses. He has written for numerous financial publications, hosted national podcasts and been seen on national television. He is acknowledged as a thought leader on personal financial management, retirement planning, investments and life insurance. Harry is a graduate of Drexel University in Philadelphia, Pennsylvania.